PRENTICE HALL MATHEMATICS

PRE-ALGEBRA

Study Guide & Practice Workbook

PEARSON

Prentice Hall

Needham, Massachusetts
Upper Saddle River, New Jersey

ISBN: 0-13-125454-5
19 20 V004 12 11 10

Study Guide & Practice Workbook

Contents

Answers appear in the back of each Grab & Go File.

Chapter 1

Reteaching and Practice 1-1 1
Reteaching and Practice 1-2 3
Reteaching and Practice 1-3 5
Reteaching and Practice 1-4 7
Reteaching and Practice 1-5 9
Reteaching and Practice 1-6 11
Reteaching and Practice 1-7 13
Reteaching and Practice 1-8 15
Reteaching and Practice 1-9 17
Reteaching and Practice 1-10 19

Chapter 2

Reteaching and Practice 2-1 21
Reteaching and Practice 2-2 23
Reteaching and Practice 2-3 25
Reteaching and Practice 2-4 27
Reteaching and Practice 2-5 29
Reteaching and Practice 2-6 31
Reteaching and Practice 2-7 33
Reteaching and Practice 2-8 35
Reteaching and Practice 2-9 37
Reteaching and Practice 2-10 39

Chapter 3

Reteaching and Practice 3-1 41
Reteaching and Practice 3-2 43
Reteaching and Practice 3-3 45
Reteaching and Practice 3-4 47
Reteaching and Practice 3-5 49
Reteaching and Practice 3-6 51
Reteaching and Practice 3-7 53
Reteaching and Practice 3-8 55

Chapter 4

Reteaching and Practice 4-1 57
Reteaching and Practice 4-2 59
Reteaching and Practice 4-3 61
Reteaching and Practice 4-4 63
Reteaching and Practice 4-5 65
Reteaching and Practice 4-6 67
Reteaching and Practice 4-7 69
Reteaching and Practice 4-8 71
Reteaching and Practice 4-9 73

Chapter 5

Reteaching and Practice 5-1 75
Reteaching and Practice 5-2 77
Reteaching and Practice 5-3 79
Reteaching and Practice 5-4 81
Reteaching and Practice 5-5 83
Reteaching and Practice 5-6 85
Reteaching and Practice 5-7 87
Reteaching and Practice 5-8 89
Reteaching and Practice 5-9 91

Chapter 6

Reteaching and Practice 6-1 93
Reteaching and Practice 6-2 95
Reteaching and Practice 6-3 97
Reteaching and Practice 6-4 99
Reteaching and Practice 6-5 101
Reteaching and Practice 6-6 103
Reteaching and Practice 6-7 105
Reteaching and Practice 6-8 107
Reteaching and Practice 6-9 109
Reteaching and Practice 6-10 111

Contents (cont.)

Chapter 7

Reteaching and Practice 7-1 113
Reteaching and Practice 7-2 115
Reteaching and Practice 7-3 117
Reteaching and Practice 7-4 119
Reteaching and Practice 7-5 121
Reteaching and Practice 7-6 123
Reteaching and Practice 7-7 125
Reteaching and Practice 7-8 127

Chapter 8

Reteaching and Practice 8-1 129
Reteaching and Practice 8-2 131
Reteaching and Practice 8-3 133
Reteaching and Practice 8-4 135
Reteaching and Practice 8-5 137
Reteaching and Practice 8-6 139
Reteaching and Practice 8-7 141
Reteaching and Practice 8-8 143

Chapter 9

Reteaching and Practice 9-1 145
Reteaching and Practice 9-2 147
Reteaching and Practice 9-3 149
Reteaching and Practice 9-4 151
Reteaching and Practice 9-5 153
Reteaching and Practice 9-6 155
Reteaching and Practice 9-7 157
Reteaching and Practice 9-8 159
Reteaching and Practice 9-9 161
Reteaching and Practice 9-10 163

Chapter 10

Reteaching and Practice 10-1 165
Reteaching and Practice 10-2 167
Reteaching and Practice 10-3 169
Reteaching and Practice 10-4 171
Reteaching and Practice 10-5 173
Reteaching and Practice 10-6 175

Reteaching and Practice 10-7 177
Reteaching and Practice 10-8 179
Reteaching and Practice 10-9 181

Chapter 11

Reteaching and Practice 11-1 183
Reteaching and Practice 11-2 185
Reteaching and Practice 11-3 187
Reteaching and Practice 11-4 189
Reteaching and Practice 11-5 191
Reteaching and Practice 11-6 193
Reteaching and Practice 11-7 195

Chapter 12

Reteaching and Practice 12-1 197
Reteaching and Practice 12-2 199
Reteaching and Practice 12-3 201
Reteaching and Practice 12-4 203
Reteaching and Practice 12-5 205
Reteaching and Practice 12-6 207
Reteaching and Practice 12-7 209
Reteaching and Practice 12-8 211
Reteaching and Practice 12-9 213

Chapter 13

Reteaching and Practice 13-1 215
Reteaching and Practice 13-2 217
Reteaching and Practice 13-3 219
Reteaching and Practice 13-4 221
Reteaching and Practice 13-5 223
Reteaching and Practice 13-6 225
Reteaching and Practice 13-7 227
Reteaching and Practice 13-8 229

Reteaching 1-1 Variables and Expressions

A *variable* is a letter that stands for a number.

Thomas needs $2 to ride the bus to Videoland. How much can he spend on video games for each amount in the table?

Thomas Has	Thomas Can Spend	
	Expression	Amount
$5	5 − 2	$3
$7	7 − 2	$5
$10	10 − 2	$8
d	d − 2	d − 2

The letter d is a variable that stands for the amount of money Thomas has. The expression $d - 2$ is a *variable expression*. It has a variable (d), a numeral (2), and an operation symbol (−).

Videoland tokens cost one dollar for 4. How many tokens can Jennifer buy for each amount of money in the table?

	Jennifer Has	Tokens Jennifer Can Buy	
		Expression	Amount
1.	$5		
2.	$8		
3.	$6		
4.	d dollars		

Write a variable expression for each word phrase.

5. h divided by 7

_____

6. j decreased by 9

_____

7. twice x

_____

8. two more than y

_____

9. the quotient of 42 and a number s

_____

10. the product of a number d and 16

_____

Practice 1-1 Variables and Expressions

Write an expression for each quantity.

1. the value in cents of 5 quarters _____

2. the value in cents of q quarters _____

3. the number of months in 7 years _____

4. the number of months in y years _____

5. the number of gallons in 21 quarts _____

6. the number of gallons in q quarts _____

Write a variable expression for each word phrase.

7. 9 less than k

   _____

8. m divided by 6

   _____

9. twice x

   _____

10. 4 more than twice x

    _____

11. the sum of eighteen and b

    _____

12. three times the quantity 2 plus a

    _____

Tell whether each expression is a numerical expression or a variable expression. For a variable expression, name the variable.

13. $4d$ _____

14. $74 + 8$ _____

15. $\frac{4(9)}{6}$ _____

16. $14 - p$ _____

17. $5k - 9$ _____

18. $3 + 3 + 3 + 3$ _____

19. $19 + 3(12)$ _____

20. $25 - 9 + x$ _____

The room temperature is c degrees centigrade. Write a word phrase for each expression.

21. $c + 15$

    _____

22. $c - 7$

    _____

Reteaching 1-2 *The Order of Operations*

Simplify $\frac{18 + 4}{2} - 3(10 \cdot 2 - 3 \cdot 6)$

$\frac{18 + 4}{2} - 3(10 \cdot 2 - 3 \cdot 6)$	Work inside grouping symbols first.
$= \frac{22}{2} - 3(10 \cdot 2 - 3 \cdot 6)$	A fraction bar is a grouping symbol.
$= 11 - 3(10 \cdot 2 - 3 \cdot 6)$	Divide the fraction.
$= 11 - 3(20 - 18)$	Multiply within the parentheses.
$= 11 - 3(2)$	Subtract within the parentheses.
$= 11 - 6$	Multiply.
$= 5$	Subtract.

Simplify each expression.

1. $8 + 2 \times 7$

_____

2. $16 \div 2 - 5$

_____

3. $\frac{8 + 12}{5}$

_____

4. $4 - 24 \div 8$

_____

5. $3 + 2 \cdot 5 - 4$

_____

6. $15 - 2(5 - 2)$

_____

7. $9 \cdot 3 + 2 \cdot 5$

_____

8. $12 \div 4 - 6 \div 3$

_____

9. $5(2 + 4) + 15 \div (9 - 6)$

_____

10. $3 \cdot 2 + 16 \div 4 - 3$

_____

11. $(18 + 7) \div (3 + 2)$

_____

12. $3[8 - 3 \cdot 2 + 4(5 - 2)]$

_____

13. $4 \cdot 9 + 8 \div 2 - 6 \cdot 5$

_____

14. $[7 + 3 \cdot 2 + 8] \div 7$

_____

15. $53 - [3(8 + 2) + 5(9 - 5)]$

_____

16. $(20 + 22) \div 6 + 1$

_____

17. $2[9(6 - 5)]$

_____

18. $5 + 3 \cdot 4 - 8 + 2 \cdot 7$

_____

Name _____ Class _____ Date _____

Simplify each expression.

1. $3 + 15 - 5 \cdot 2$ _____

2. $5 \cdot 6 + 2 \cdot 4$ _____

3. $48 \div 8 - 1$ _____

4. $68 - 12 \div 2 \div 3$ _____

5. $6(2 + 7)$ _____

6. $25 - (6 \cdot 4)$ _____

7. $3[9 - (6 - 3)] - 10$ _____

8. $60 \div (3 + 12)$ _____

9. $4 - 2 + 6 \cdot 2$ _____

10. $18 \div (5 - 2)$ _____

11. $\frac{16 + 24}{30 - 22}$ _____

12. $2[4(9 - 7) + 1]$ _____

13. $(8 \div 8 + 2 + 11) \div 2$ _____

14. $9 + 3 \cdot 4$ _____

15. $18 \div 3 \cdot 5 - 4$ _____

16. $10 + 28 \div 14 - 5$ _____

Insert grouping symbols to make each number sentence true.

17. $3 + 5 \cdot 8 = 64$

18. $4 \cdot 6 - 2 + 7 = 23$

19. $10 \div 3 + 2 \cdot 4 = 8$

20. $3 + 6 \cdot 2 = 18$

A city park has two walkways with a grassy area in the center, as shown in the diagram.

21. Write an expression for the area of the sidewalks, using subtraction.

    _____

22. Write an expression for the area of the sidewalks, using addition.

    _____

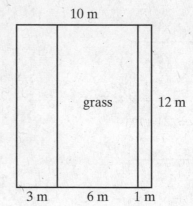

Compare. Use >, <, or = to complete each statement.

23. $(24 - 8) \div 4$ ☐ $24 - 8 \div 4$

24. $3 \cdot (4 - 2) \cdot 5$ ☐ $3 \cdot 4 - 2 \cdot 5$

25. $(22 + 8) \div 2$ ☐ $22 + 8 \div 2$

26. $20 \div 2 + 8 \cdot 2$ ☐ $20 \div (2 + 8) \cdot 2$

27. $11 \cdot 4 - 2$ ☐ $11 \cdot (4 - 2)$

28. $(7 \cdot 3) - (4 \cdot 2)$ ☐ $7 \cdot 3 - 4 \cdot 2$

Reteaching 1-3 *Evaluating Expressions*

Evaluate $a(b + 4) - c$, for $a = 2$, $b = 5$, and $c = 12$.

$a(b + 4) - c$

$= 2(5 + 4) - 12$	Replace the variables.
$= 2(9) - 12$	Work within grouping symbols.
$= 18 - 12$	Multiply.
$= 6$	Subtract.

Evaluate each expression.

1. $2n - 7$, for $n = 8$

2. $4ab$, for $a = 2$ and $b = 5$

3. $\frac{x + y}{3}$, for $x = 7$ and $y = 8$

4. $2(m + n)$, for $m = 3$ and $n = 2$

5. $37 - 5h$, for $h = 7$

6. $\frac{6}{a} + b$, for $a = 3$ and $b = 7$

7. $4x + 5y - 3z$, for $x = 3$, $y = 4$, and $z = 2$ _____

8. $15a - 2(b + c)$, for $a = 2$, $b = 3$, and $c = 4$ _____

9. $7p + q(3 + r)$, for $p = 3$, $q = 2$, and $r = 1$ _____

10. $\frac{36}{j} - 4(k + l)$, for $j = 2$, $k = 1$, and $l = 3$ _____

11. $x + 3y - 4(z - 3)$, for $x = 4$, $y = 6$, and $z = 5$ _____

12. $(4 + d) - e(9 - f)$, for $d = 7$, $e = 4$, $f = 8$ _____

13. $3a - 2b + b(6 - 2)$, for $a = 4$, $b = 2$ _____

14. $r(p + 3) + q(p - 1)$, for $p = 7$, $q = 4$, $r = 3$ _____

Practice 1-3 Evaluating Expressions

Evaluate each expression.

1. xy, for $x = 3$ and $y = 5$ _____
2. $24 - p \cdot 5$, for $p = 4$ _____

3. $5a + b$, for $a = 6$ and $b = 3$ _____
4. $6x$, for $x = 3$ _____

5. $9 - k$, for $k = 2$ _____
6. $63 \div p$, for $p = 7$ _____

7. $2 + n$, for $n = 3$ _____
8. $3m$, for $m = 11$ _____

9. $10 - r + 5$, for $r = 9$ _____

10. $m + n \div 6$, for $m = 12$ and $n = 18$ _____

11. $1{,}221 \div x$, for $x = 37$ _____
12. $10 - x$, for $x = 3$ _____

13. $4m + 3$, for $m = 5$ _____
14. $35 - 3x$, for $x = 10$ _____

15. $851 - p$, for $p = 215$ _____

16. $18a - 9b$, for $a = 12$ and $b = 15$ _____

17. $3ab - c$, for $a = 4$, $b = 2$, and $c = 5$ _____

18. $\frac{ab}{2} + 4c$, for $a = 6$, $b = 5$, and $c = 3$ _____

19. $\frac{rst}{3}$, for $r = 9$, $s = 2$, and $t = 4$ _____ .

20. $x(y + 5) - z$, for $x = 3$, $y = 2$, and $z = 7$ _____

21. Elliot is 58 years old.

    a. Write an expression for the number of years by which Elliot's age

    exceeds that of his daughter, who is y years old. _____

    b. If his daughter is 25, how much older is Elliot? _____

22. A tree grows 5 in. each year.

    a. Write an expression for the tree's height after x years. _____

    b. When the tree is 36 years old, how tall will it be? _____

Name _____ Class _____ Date _____

Reteaching 1-4 *Integers and Absolute Value*

Compare. Use >, <, or = to complete each statement.

a. -4 ☐ -2

Graph -4 and -2 on the number line.

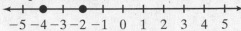

A number on the left is less than a number on the right.
Thus, -4 is less than -2.
$-4 < -2$

b. $|-4|$ ☐ $|-2|$

The *absolute value* of a number is its distance from zero on the number line.

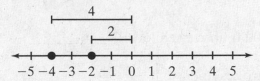

Thus $|-4| = 4$ and $|-2| = 2$.
Since $4 > 2$, $|-4| > |-2|$

Compare. Use >, <, or = to complete each statement.

1. -3 ☐ -2 **2.** -5 ☐ 1 **3.** 0 ☐ -2

4. 1 ☐ 0 **5.** 1 ☐ -1 **6.** -5 ☐ -3

7. $|-3|$ ☐ 0 **8.** $|-2|$ ☐ $|-5|$ **9.** $|-3|$ ☐ 2

10. $|-6|$ ☐ 6 **11.** $|3|$ ☐ $|-2|$ **12.** $|-7|$ ☐ 0

13. -3 ☐ $|-3|$ **14.** 4 ☐ $|-2|$ **15.** $|-2|$ ☐ 3

16. $|-5|$ ☐ 3 **17.** $|8|$ ☐ $|-8|$ **18.** -6 ☐ -4

19. 5 ☐ $|-4|$ **20.** -3 ☐ -5 **21.** $|2|$ ☐ $|-3|$

22. $|-1|$ ☐ $|1|$ **23.** $|-3|$ ☐ $|-1|$ **24.** -1 ☐ 2

Name _____ Class _____ Date _____

Practice 1-4 *Integers and Absolute Value*

Graph each set of numbers on a number line. Then order the numbers from least to greatest.

1. $-4, -8, 5$

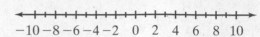

_____

2. $3, -3, -2$

_____

3. $0, -9, -5$

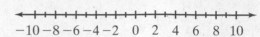

_____

4. $-7, -1, -6$

_____

Write an integer to represent each quantity.

5. 5 degrees below zero _____

6. 2,000 ft above sea level _____

7. a loss of 12 yd _____

8. 7 strokes under par _____

Simplify each expression.

9. the opposite of -15 _____

10. $|-9|$ _____

11. $-|-25|$ _____

12. the opposite of $|-8|$ _____

13. $-|-31|$ _____

14. $|847|$ _____

Write the integer represented by each point on the number line.

15. A _____

16. B _____

17. C _____

18. D _____

19. E _____

Compare. Use $>$, $<$, or $=$ to complete each statement.

20. $-3 \boxed{} 4$

21. $5 \boxed{} 1$

22. $-2 \boxed{} -6$

23. $7 \boxed{} |8|$

24. $|-2| \boxed{} |2|$

25. $|-1| \boxed{} -6$

26. $|4| \boxed{} |-5|$

27. $0 \boxed{} |-7|$

Pre-Algebra Chapter 1

Reteaching 1-5 Adding Integers

Use tiles and the rules for adding integers to find each sum.

a. −4 + −3

Four negative tiles plus 3 negative tiles gives 7 negative tiles.
−4 + −3 = −7
The sum of two negative integers is negative.

b. −8 + 3

Remove zero
pairs

Since the signs of the integers are different, you must remove zero pairs.
The number of tiles left is the number of negative tiles |−8| minus the
number of positive tiles |3|. Thus, you can always subtract the absolute
values of the numbers to find how many tiles will be left.

|−8| − |3| = 5

Since there are more negative tiles than positive tiles, |−8| > |3|, there
are negative tiles left after you subtract zero pairs. Thus, the sum is
negative.

−8 + 3 = −5

Use rules or tiles to find each sum.

1. 9 + (−12)　　　　**2.** −4 + 10　　　　**3.** −1 + (−8)

_____　　　_____　　　_____

4. −6 + (−11)　　　**5.** −5 + 15　　　　**6.** 2 + (−14)

_____　　　_____　　　_____

7. (−3) + (−6)　　　**8.** −(−2) + 9　　　**9.** (−2) + (−4)

_____　　　_____　　　_____

10. −5 + 4　　　　　**11.** 7 + (−2)　　　　**12.** 16 + (−6)

_____　　　_____　　　_____

Practice 1-5 Adding Integers

Write a numerical expression for each of the following. Then find the sum.

1. climb up 26 steps, then climb down 9 steps

_____

2. earn $100, spend $62, earn $35, spend $72

_____

Find each sum.

3. $-8 + (-3)$

4. $6 + (-6)$

5. $-12 + (-17)$

6. $9 + (-11)$

7. $-4 + (-6)$

8. $18 + (-17)$

9. $-8 + 8 + (-11)$

10. $12 + (-7) + 3 + (-8)$

11. $-15 + 7 + 15$

12. $0 + (-11)$

13. $6 + (-5) + (-4)$

14. $-5 + (-16) + 5 + 8 + 16$

Without adding, tell whether each sum is positive, negative, or zero.

15. $192 + (-129)$

16. $-417 + (-296)$

17. $-175 + 87$

Evaluate each expression for $n = -12$.

18. $n + 8$

19. $n + (-5)$

20. $12 + n$

Compare. Write >, <, or = to complete each statement.

21. $-7 + 5 \boxed{} 3 + (-6)$

22. $4 + (-9) \boxed{} 6 + (-7) + (-4)$

23. An elevator went up 15 floors, down 9 floors, up 11 floors, and down 19

floors. Find the net change. _____

24. The price of a share of stock started the day at $37. During the day it went down $3, up $1, down $7, and up $4. What was the price of a share at the end of the day?

_____

Reteaching 1-6 *Subtracting Integers*

a. Find $-7 - (-3)$ and $-7 + 3$. Compare.

$-7 - (-3)$ $-7 + 3$

Start with 7 negative   Remove zero pairs.
tiles and take away
3 negative tiles.

With both you start with 7 negative tiles. Taking away 3 negative tiles
has the same effect as adding 3 positive tiles and removing zero pairs.
$-7 - (-3) = -7 + 3 = -4$

b. Find $-4 - 2$ and $-4 + (-2)$. Compare.

$-4 - 2$ $-4 + (-2)$

With both you start with 4 negative tiles. Adding two zero pairs and
taking away two positive tiles has the same effect as adding two negative
tiles.
$-4 - 2 = -4 + (-2) = -6$

**Use rules for subtracting integers to find each difference. Use tiles
to help.**

1. $-5 - (-3) = -5 +$ _____ = _____

2. $-8 - 6 = -8 +$ _____ = _____

3. $3 - (-9) = 3 +$ _____ = _____

4. $-2 - (-7) = -2 +$ _____ = _____

5. $4 - 10 = 4 +$ _____ = _____

6. $1 - (-6) = 1 +$ _____ = _____

7. $-9 - 5 = -9 +$ _____ = _____

8. $-6 - (-2) = -6 +$ _____ = _____

9. $7 - 8 = 7 +$ _____ = _____

Practice 1-6 *Subtracting Integers*

Use rules to find each difference.

1. $8 - 12$

2. $13 - 6$

3. $9 - (-12)$

_____

4. $57 - 39$

5. $-173 - 162$

6. $71 - (123)$

_____

7. $51 - 89$

8. $-222 - (-117)$

9. $843 - 677$

_____

10. $-98 - 183$

11. $366 - (-429)$

12. $-83 - (-48) - 65$

_____

Find each difference.

13. $6 - 9$

14. $14 - 8$

15. $-15 - 3$

_____

16. $-25 - 25$

17. $-16 - (-16)$

18. $32 - (-17) - 32$

_____

Round each number. Then estimate each sum or difference.

19. $-57 + (-98)$

20. $448 - 52$

21. $-191 + (-511)$

_____

22. $-361 - (-58)$

23. $888 + 1,177$

24. $-484 - 1,695$

_____

Write a numerical expression for each phrase. Then simplify.

25. A balloon goes up 2,300 ft, then goes down 600 ft.

_____

26. You lose $50, then spend $35.

_____

27. The Glasers had $317 in their checking account. They wrote checks for $74, $132, and $48. What is their checking account balance?

_____

Reteaching 1-7 *Inductive Reasoning*

The sum of two numbers is always at least as great as either number. Is the statement correct or incorrect? If incorrect, give a counterexample.

Try some examples.

$2 + 8 = 10$ $10 \geq 8$ and $10 \geq 2$

$365 + 241 = 606$ $606 \geq 365$ and $606 \geq 241$

The conjecture seems correct. Try different kinds of numbers. Although the numbers in the second trial are much larger than those in the first, all are whole numbers. Try zero, fractions, and negative numbers.

$56 + 0 = 56$ $56 \geq 56$ and $56 \geq 0$

$\frac{3}{8} + \frac{1}{8} = \frac{1}{2}$ $\frac{1}{2} \geq \frac{3}{8}$ and $\frac{1}{2} \geq \frac{1}{8}$

$-4 + 7 = 3$ $3 \geq -4$ but 3 is not at least as great as 7

The conjecture is incorrect and $-4 + 7 = 3$ is a counterexample.

Is each conjecture correct or incorrect? If incorrect, give a counterexample.

1. The difference of two numbers is less than or equal to each number.

_____

2. The sum of two negative numbers is always less than each number.

_____

3. The sum of 5 and any positive integer is divisible by 5.

_____

4. A number is divisible by 10 if its last digit is 0.

_____

5. The sum of a number and its absolute value is always 0.

_____

6. The next number in the pattern 2, 4, 8, . . . is 10.

_____

7. Every even number is divisible by 4.

_____

8. The next number in the pattern 5, 3, 1, . . . is -1.

_____

◼ Practice 1-7 *Inductive Reasoning*

Write a rule for each pattern. Find the next three numbers in each pattern.

1. 3, 6, 9, 12, 15, _____, _____, _____   **2.** 1, 2, 4, 8, 16, _____, _____, _____

   Rule: _____   Rule: _____

   _____   _____

3. 6, 7, 14, 15, 30, 31, _____, _____, _____   **4.** 34, 27, 20, 13, 6, _____, _____, _____

   Rule: _____   Rule: _____

   _____   _____

Is each statement correct or incorrect? If it is incorrect, give a counterexample.

5. All roses are red.

   _____

6. A number is divisible by 4 if its last two digits are divisible by 4.

   _____

7. The difference of two numbers is always less than at least one of the numbers.

   _____

Describe the next figure in each pattern. Then draw the figure.

8.

   _____

9.

   _____

10.

   _____

   _____

11.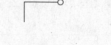

   _____

   _____

Name _____ Class _____ Date _____

Reteaching 1-8 Look for a Pattern

Margarita learned to dig clams over her vacation and got steadily better at finding clams each day. On the first day she found 2 clams, on the second day 5 clams, and on the third day 8. If she continued to improve at the same rate, how many clams did she find on the sixth day?

Make a table to organize the numbers. Then look for a pattern.

Day	1	2	3	4	5	6
Clams	2	5	8	11	14	17
More Than Day Before	0	3	3	3	3	3

Margarita found 17 clams on the sixth day.

Phillipe got steadily better at playing ping pong on his vacation. The table shows the number of games he won the first three days. If he continued to improve at the same rate, how many games would he win on the sixth day?

1. Complete the table.

Day	1	2	3	4	5	6
Games Won	3	5	7			
More Than Day Before	0					

2. Solve the problem.

Jennifer improved her bike riding distance steadily while preparing for a race. The table shows the distance in miles she rode during the first three weeks of training. If she continues to improve at the same rate, how many miles will she be able to ride in the sixth week? How many more miles did she ride in week 6 than she rode in week 5?

3. Complete the table.

Week	1	2	3	4	5	6
Miles Traveled	3	4	6	9		
More Than Week Before	0					

4. Solve the problems.

_____

_____

Practice 1-8 Look for a Pattern

Solve by looking for a pattern.

1. Each row in a window display of floppy disk cartons contains two more boxes than the row above. The first row has one box.
   a. Complete the table.

Row Number	1	2	3	4	5	6
Boxes in the Row						
Total Boxes in the Display						

   b. Describe the pattern in the numbers you wrote.

   _____

   _____

   c. Find the number of rows in a display containing the given number of boxes.

   81 _____   144 _____   400 _____

   d. Describe how you can use the number of boxes in the display to calculate the number of rows.

   _____

   _____

2. A computer multiplied nine 100 times. You can use patterns to find the ones digit of the product.

   $$9 \times 9 \times 9 \times 9 \times \cdots \times 9$$

   100 times

   a. Find the ones digit when nine is multiplied:

   1 time _____   2 times _____   3 times _____   4 times _____

   b. Describe the pattern. _____

   _____

   _____

   c. What is the ones digit of the computer's product? _____

3. Use the method of Exercise 2 to find the ones digit of the product when 4 is multiplied by itself 100 times. _____

Reteaching 1-9 Multiplying and Dividing Integers

Multiplying and dividing integers is very similar to multiplying and dividing whole numbers. Just remember the two basic rules for determining the sign of the product or quotient.

Rule 1: The product or quotient of two integers with the *same sign* is positive.

Rule 2: The product or quotient of two integers with *opposite signs* is negative.

Find each product or quotient.

a. $5 \cdot 7$

$5 \cdot 7 = 35$

↑ ↑

Same sign (both +)

b. $-2(-3)$

$-2(-3) = 6$

↑ ↑

Same sign (both −)

c. $15 \div 3$

$15 \div 3 = 5$

↑ ↑

Same sign (both +)

d. $-40 \div (-10)$

$-40 \div (-10) = 4$

↑ ↑

Same sign (both −)

e. $-5 \cdot 7$

$-5 \cdot 7 = -35$

↑ ↑

Opposite signs (−, +)

f. $2(-3)$

$2(-3) = -6$

↑ ↑

Opposite signs (+, −)

g. $-15 \div 3$

$-15 \div 3 = -5$

↑ ↑

Opposite signs (−, +)

h. $40 \div (-10)$

$40 \div (-10) = -4$

↑ ↑

Opposite signs (+, −)

Complete the table. The first row has been done for you.

		Same or Opposite Sign?	Sign of Product or Quotient	Product or Quotient
	$-5 \cdot 12$	Opposite	Negative	-60
1.	$-91 \div (-13)$			
2.	$6 \cdot 8$			
3.	$72 \div -9$			
4.	$-3(-6)$			
5.	$-18 \div 2$			
6.	$11 \cdot (-5)$			
7.	$52 \div 4$			
8.	$-12(6)$			

Practice 1-9 Multiplying and Dividing Integers

Use repeated addition, patterns, or rules to find each product or quotient.

1. $23 \cdot 16$

2. $8 \cdot 7(-6)$

3. $-17 \cdot 3$

_____   _____   _____

4. $-24 \div 4$

5. $-65 \div 5$

6. $117 \div (-1)$

_____   _____   _____

7. $-30 \div (-6)$

8. $-21 \div (-3)$

9. $63 \div (-21)$

_____   _____   _____

10. $5(-1)(-9)$

11. $-6(-3) \cdot 2$

12. $-3 \cdot 7(-2)$

_____   _____   _____

13. $\frac{1,512}{-42}$

14. $\frac{-4,875}{-65}$

15. $\frac{-15(-3)}{-9}$

_____   _____   _____

Compare. Use >, <, or = to complete each statement.

16. $-7(5)$ ☐ $-6 \cdot (-6)$

17. $-20 \cdot (-5)$ ☐ $10 \cdot |-10|$

18. $3(-6)$ ☐ $-3(6)$

19. $121 \div (-11)$ ☐ $-45 \div (-6)$

20. $-40 \div 8$ ☐ $40 \div (-8)$

21. $-54 \div 9$ ☐ $21 \div (-3)$

For each group, find the average.

22. temperatures: $6°, -15°, -24°, 3°, -25°$ _____

23. bank balances: $\$52, -\$7, \$20, -\$63, -\$82$ _____

24. stock price changes: $\$6, -\$6, -\$9, \$1, \$3$ _____

25. golf scores: $-2, 0, 3, -2, -3, 1, -4$ _____

26. elevations (ft): $-120, 168, -60, -42, -36$ _____

Write a multiplication or division sentence to answer the question.

27. The temperature dropped $4°$ each hour for 3 hours. What was the total change in temperature?

_____

Reteaching 1-10 *The Coordinate Plane*

Write the coordinates of point A.

Point A is 3 units to the right of the y-axis. So
the x-coordinate is 3. It is 4 units below the x-axis.
So the y-coordinate is -4. The coordinates of
point A are $(3, -4)$.

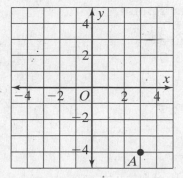

In which quadrant is point A located?

Compare the point to the diagram. Point A is in
the fourth quadrant.

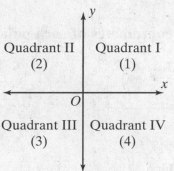

Write the coordinates of each point.

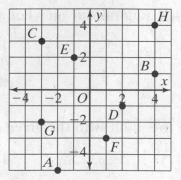

1. A _____	**2.** B _____
3. C _____	**4.** D _____
5. E _____	**6.** F _____
7. G _____	**8.** H _____

In which quadrant does each point lie?

9. A _____	**10.** B _____
11. C _____	**12.** D _____
13. E _____	**14.** F _____
15. G _____	**16.** H _____

Practice 1-10 The Coordinate Plane

Graph each point.

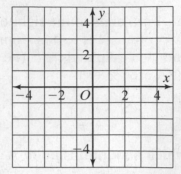

1. $A(-2, 2)$
2. $B(0, 3)$
3. $C(-3, 0)$
4. $D(2, 3)$
5. $E(-1, -2)$
6. $F(4, -2)$

Write the coordinates of each point.

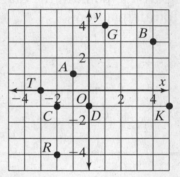

7. A _____
8. B _____

9. C _____
10. D _____

In which quadrant or on what axis does each point fall?

11. A _____
12. B _____

13. C _____
14. D _____

Name the point with the given coordinates.

15. $(1, 4)$ _____
16. $(-3, 0)$ _____

17. $(5, -1)$ _____
18. $(-2, -4)$ _____

Complete using *positive*, *negative*, or *zero*.

19. In Quadrant II, x is _____ and y is _____.

20. In Quadrant III, x is _____ and y is _____.

21. On the y-axis x is _____.

22. On the x-axis y is _____.

Reteaching 2-1 Properties of Numbers

Properties of numbers help make mental computations easier.

Use mental math to simplify $1.84 + $.76 + $.16.

Since $0.84 + 0.16 = 1$, it is easier to add $1.84 and $.16 first.

$1.84 + 0.76 + 0.16$

$= 1.84 + (0.16 + 0.76)$	Use the commutative property of addition.
$= (1.84 + 0.16) + 0.76$	Use the associative property of addition.
$= 2.00 + 0.76$	Add within parentheses.
$= 2.76	Add.

Use mental math to simplify $5 \cdot 13 \cdot 20 \cdot 2$.

Since $5 \cdot 20 = 100$, it is easier to multiply 5 and 20 first.

$5 \cdot 13 \cdot 20 \cdot 2$

$= 5 \cdot (20 \cdot 13) \cdot 2$	Use the commutative property of multiplication.
$= (5 \cdot 20) \cdot (13 \cdot 2)$	Use the associative property of multiplication.
$= 100 \cdot 26$	Multiply within parentheses.
$= 2,600$	Multiply.

Use mental math to simplify each expression.

1. $198 + 15 + 302$

_____

2. $16 + 27 + (-16)$

_____

3. $4 \cdot 7 \cdot 25$

_____

4. $2 \cdot 6 \cdot 5$

_____

5. $18 + (-8) + 11$

_____

6. $5 \cdot 9 \cdot 8$

_____

7. $21 + 4 + (-1)$

_____

8. $1,242 + 125 + 58$

_____

9. $50 \cdot 13 \cdot 2$

_____

10. $(-209) + 576 + (-91)$

_____

11. $17 + 9 + 13 + 6$

_____

12. $125 \cdot 353 \cdot 8$

_____

Practice 2-1 *Properties of Numbers*

Simplify each expression using mental math.

1. $4 \cdot 13 \cdot 25$

2. $700 + 127 + 300$

3. $68 + 85 + 32$

_____

_____

_____

4. $2 \cdot 3 \cdot 4 \cdot 5$

5. $-14 + 71 + 29 + (-86)$

6. $125 \cdot 9 \cdot 8$

_____

_____

_____

7. $20 \cdot 7 \cdot 5$

8. $217 + 545 - 17$

9. $39 + 27 + 11$

_____

_____

_____

10. $4 \cdot 12 \cdot 250$

11. $19 + 0 + (-9)$

12. $-6 \cdot 1 \cdot 30$

_____

_____

_____

Write the letter of the property shown.

13. $14(mn) = (14m)n$ _____

14. $19 + 11 = 11 + 19$ _____

15. $k \cdot 1 = k$ _____

16. $(x + y) + z = x + (y + z)$ _____

17. $65t = t(65)$ _____

18. $p = 0 + p$ _____

19. $n = 1 \cdot n$ _____

20. $(x + p) + (r + t) = (r + t) + (x + p)$ _____

21. $(h + 0) + 4 = h + 4$ _____

22. $x + yz = x + zy$ _____

a. commutative property of addition
b. associative property of addition
c. commutative property of multiplication
d. associative property of multiplication
e. additive identity
f. multiplicative identity

Evaluate each expression using mental math.

23. $x(yz)$, for $x = 8, y = -9, z = 5$ _____

24. $q + r + s$, for $q = 46, r = 19, s = 54$ _____

25. $a(b)(-c)$, for $a = 7, b = -2, c = 15$ _____

▬ *Reteaching 2-2* *The Distributive Property*

According to the Distributive Property, you distribute or "pass out" a multiplication to each part of a sum or difference in parentheses.

In $2(a + b) = 2a + 2b$, we "pass out" the 2 by multiplying it by both the a and the b.

Multiply $6(x - 9)$.
$$6(x - 9) = 6x - 6(9)$$
$$= 6x - 54$$

Multiply $(4 - h)(-3)$.
$$(4 - h)(-3) = 4(-3) - h(-3)$$
$$= -12 - (-3h)$$
$$= -12 + 3h$$
$$= 3h - 12$$

Complete with the appropriate number or variable.

1. $12(5 + 9) = 12 \cdot 5 + \underline{\hspace{1cm}} \cdot 9$

2. $(3 - 8)7 = \underline{\hspace{1cm}} \cdot 7 - 8 \cdot \underline{\hspace{1cm}}$

3. $z(a - b - c) = \underline{\hspace{1cm}} \cdot a - z \cdot \underline{\hspace{1cm}} - \underline{\hspace{1cm}} \cdot \underline{\hspace{1cm}}$

4. $[14 + (-3)]7 = 14 \cdot \underline{\hspace{1cm}} + \underline{\hspace{1cm}} \cdot 7$

5. $p[(-3) + n] = p \cdot \underline{\hspace{1cm}} + \underline{\hspace{1cm}} \cdot \underline{\hspace{1cm}}$

Multiply each expression.

6. $4(x + 5) = $ _____

7. $(6 - m)(-4) = $ _____

8. $s(-6 + t) = $ _____

9. $8(j - 2k + l) = $ _____

10. $(z - 4)(-5) = $ _____

11. $9[(-7) - y] = $ _____

Practice 2-2 *The Distributive Property*

Write an expression using parentheses for each model. Then multiply.

1. ⌸⌸⌸⌸⬚ ⌸⌸⌸⌸⬚ ⌸⌸⌸⌸⬚   2. ⌸⌸⌸⌸⬚ ⌸⌸⌸⌸⬚

_____   _____

Multiply each expression.

3. $6(h - 4)$ _____   4. $(p + 3)5$ _____

5. $-3(x + 8)$ _____   6. $(4 - y)(-9)$ _____

7. $2(7n - 11)$ _____   8. $-10(-a + 5)$ _____

Use the distributive property to simplify.

9. $98 \cdot 7$ _____

10. $9 \cdot 28$ _____

11. $78 \cdot 8$ _____

12. $7(2,009)$ _____

13. $899 \cdot 5$ _____

14. $30 \cdot 105$ _____

15. $8 \cdot 5 - 12 \cdot 5$ _____

16. $7 \cdot 10 + 7(-3)$ _____

17. $-4(3) + (-4)(6)$ _____

18. $6(8) + 6(-2)$ _____

Solve using mental math.

19. A shipping container holds 144 boxes. How many boxes can be shipped

in 4 containers? _____

Reteaching 2-3 Simplifying Variable Expressions

Simplify $5n + (-n - 4)(-2)$.

$5n + (-n - 4)(-2)$

$= 5n + (-n)(-2) - 4(-2)$ Use the Distributive Property.

$= 5n + 2n + 8$ Multiply. Think of $-4(-2)$ as $+(-4)(-2)$.

$= (5 + 2)n + 8$ Use the Distributive Property to combine like terms.

$= 7n + 8$ Add.

Complete each equation.

1. $9a - 7a + 5$

$= (9 - 7)$ _____ $+ 5$

$=$ _____ $a + 5$

2. $5k - 4 - 8k$

$= 5k - 8$ _____ $- 4$

$= (5 - 8)$ _____ $- 4$

$=$ _____ $- 4$

Simplify each expression.

3. $12a + 4 - 10a$

_____

4. $7 + x - 7x$

_____

5. $2(n - 4) + 3$

_____

6. $-3(a + 5) + 9$

_____

7. $5(2y + 1) - 7y$

_____

8. $2(4 - 3t) - (-3) + 2t$

_____

9. $8c + 5(c - 3)$

_____

10. $-2(-4 - 3s)$

_____

11. $q(-3) + 3(2 + q)$

_____

12. $(3 + k)(-4) - 5k$

_____

13. $(-3)(1 - 2n) + 2(n + 4)$

_____

14. $9p - 3(5p + 2) + 6$

_____

Name _____ Class _____ Date _____

Practice 2-3 Simplifying Variable Expressions

Simplify each expression.

1. $16 + 7y - 8$ **2.** $18m - 7 + 12m$ **3.** $5(3t) - 7(2t)$

_____   _____   _____

4. $2x - 9y + 7x + 20y$ **5.** $3(9k - 4) - 4(5n - 3)$ **6.** $6(g - h) - 6(g - h)$

_____   _____   _____

7. $-21(a + 2b) + 14a - 9b$ **8.** $-7a + 3(a - c) + 5c$ **9.** $-2(-5)q + (-72)(-q)$

_____   _____   _____

Name the coefficients, any like terms, and any constants.

	Coefficients	Like Terms	Constants
10. $3x + 7$	_____	_____	_____
11. $4m + (-3n) + n$	_____	_____	_____
12. $6kp + 9k + kp - 14$	_____	_____	_____
13. $-8y + 6ab + 7 - 3ba$	_____	_____	_____
14. $c + 2c + c - 5c + 1$	_____	_____	_____

Write an expression for each model. Simplify the expression.

15.

_____

16.

_____

Justify each step.

17. $5(n + 4) + 9n = (5n + 20) + 9n$ _____

$\qquad\qquad\quad = 5n + (20 + 9n)$ _____

$\qquad\qquad\quad = 5n + (9n + 20)$ _____

$\qquad\qquad\quad = (5n + 9n) + 20$ _____

$\qquad\qquad\quad = (5 + 9)n + 20$ _____

$\qquad\qquad\quad = 14n + 20$ _____

Reteaching 2-4　*Variables and Equations*

You earned $84 at $6 an hour. Let h be the number of hours you worked. Can h be 12? Can h be 14?

Write an equation.

Words　　Rate of pay · Hours worked = Total pay

Let h = hours worked.

Equation　　　6　·　　　h　=　　84

$$6h = 84$$

$$6(12) \overset{?}{=} 84 \qquad \text{Substitute 12 for } h.$$

$$72 \neq 84$$

No, you did not work 12 hours.

$$6(14) \overset{?}{=} 84 \qquad \text{Substitute 14 for } h.$$

$$84 = 84$$

Yes, you worked 14 hours.

Write an equation. Is the given value a solution?

1. You rode 180 miles at 60 miles per hour. Let t be the time it took. Can t be 4 hours?

   _____

2. Ernie scored 8 more points than Mike scored. Ernie scored 20 points. Let p be the number of points Mike scored. Can p be 12?

   _____

3. Each person in your class contributed a quart of punch for the school dance. You divided them into gallon containers and got 5 gallons. Let q be the number of quarts you started with. Could q be 20? (*Hint*: There are 4 quarts in a gallon.)

   _____

4. You typed a 600 word essay in 12 minutes. Let w be the number of words you can type in one minute. Can w be 60?

   _____

   _____

Practice 2-4 *Variables and Equations*

Is the given number a solution of the equation?

1. $9k = 10 - k; -1$ _____

2. $-7r - 15 = -2r; -3$ _____

3. $3g \div (-6) = 5 - g; -10$ _____

4. $-3p = 4p + 35; -5$ _____

5. $8 - e = 2e - 16; 8$ _____

6. $5 - 15s = 8 - 16s; 3$ _____

7. $2(x - 2) - 5x = 5(2 - x); 7$ _____

8. $6a + 3 = 3(3a - 2); 4$ _____

Is each equation true, false, or an open sentence?

9. $14 = x - 9$

_____

10. $8 + 7 = 10$

_____

11. $4 - 15 = 22 - 33$

_____

12. $5 + x = 90 \div 9 + 4$

_____

13. $-7(5 - 9) = 19 - 3(-3)$

_____

14. $6(5 - 8) = 2(10 - 1)$

_____

Write an equation for each sentence. Is each equation true, false, or an open sentence?

15. One fifth of a number n is equal to -7.

_____

16. The product of 13 and -7 is -91.

_____

17. Fifty-four divided by six equals negative nine.

_____

18. Seven less than the product of a number z and 3 is equal to 4.

_____

Write an equation. Is the given value a solution?

19. A truck driver drove 468 miles on Tuesday. That was 132 miles farther than she drove on Monday. Let d represent the distance she drove on Monday. Did she drive 600 miles on Monday?

_____

Name _____ Class _____ Date _____

Reteaching 2-5 *Solving Equations by Adding or Subtracting*

Solve $x - 9 = 2$ and $x + 8 = 3$.

Since the 9 is subtracted from x, do the inverse and add 9 to each side of the equation.

$$x - 9 = 2$$
$$x - 9 + 9 = 2 + 9$$
$$x = 11$$

In $x + 8 = 3$, 8 is added to x. So, subtract 8 from each side of the equation.

$$x + 8 = 3$$
$$x + 8 - 8 = 3 - 8$$
$$x = -5$$

Solve each equation.

1. $17 + m = 21$

_____

2. $y - 34 = 43$

_____

3. $t + 9 = -9$

_____

4. $15 = z + 6$

_____

5. $r + 7 = -16$

_____

6. $68 = p - 41$

_____

7. $144 + g = 78$

_____

8. $311 = y - 281$

_____

9. $-11 + b = -11$

_____

10. $s + 31 = 14$

_____

11. $24 = k - 2$

_____

12. $8 + f = 30$

_____

13. $37 = z - 3$

_____

14. $a + 19 = -82$

_____

15. $18 + n - 7 = 44$

_____

16. $15 = 7 + h + 14$

_____

Practice 2-5 Solving Equations by Adding or Subtracting

Use mental math to solve each equation.

1. $-52 = -52 + k$ _____

2. $837 = p + 37$ _____

3. $x - 155 = 15$ _____

4. $180 = 80 + n$ _____

5. $2{,}000 + y = 9{,}500$ _____

6. $81 = x - 19$ _____

7. $111 + f = 100$ _____

8. $w - 6 = -16$ _____

Solve each equation.

9. $m - 17 = -8$ _____

10. $k - 55 = 67$ _____

11. $-44 + n = 36$ _____

12. $-36 = p - 91$ _____

13. $x - 255 = 671$ _____

14. $19 = c - (-12)$ _____

15. $x + 14 = 21$ _____

16. $31 = p + 17$ _____

17. $-19 = k + 9$ _____

18. $87 + y = 19$ _____

19. $36 + n = 75$ _____

20. $-176 = h + (-219)$ _____

21. $41 + k = 7$ _____

22. $1{,}523 + c = 2{,}766$ _____

23. $-88 + z = 0$ _____

24. $-33 + (-7) = 29 + m$ _____

25. $t + (-2) = -66$ _____

26. $-390 + x = 11 - 67$ _____

27. The combined enrollment in the three grades at Jefferson Middle School is 977. There are 356 students in the seventh grade and 365 in the eighth grade. Write and solve an equation to find how many students are in the ninth grade.

Equation _____

Solution _____

Reteaching 2-6 Solving Equations by Multiplying or Dividing

Solve $4x = -32$.

$4x - -32$

$\frac{4x}{4} = \frac{-32}{4}$ Since 4 is multiplied by x, divide each side of the equation by 4.

$x = -8$

Solve $\frac{x}{-5} = -9$.

$\frac{x}{-5} = -9$

$-5\left(\frac{x}{-5}\right) = -5(-9)$ Since x is divided by -5, multiply each side of the equation by -5.

$x = 45$

Solve each equation.

1. $7m = 35$

2. $\frac{b}{8} = -3$

3. $90 = 10k$

4. $1 = \frac{n}{14}$

5. $100 = -20n$

6. $\frac{p}{15} = 5$

7. $-87,654y = 0$

8. $\frac{m}{4} = -12$

9. $-10a = 10$

10. $\frac{z}{-4} = 16$

11. $350t = -700$

12. $11j = 121$

13. $\frac{r}{-7} = 13$

14. $-7,650 = 10c$

15. $23 = \frac{w}{3}$

16. $125 = 25g$

Practice 2-6 Solving Equations by Multiplying or Dividing

Solve each equation.

1. $\frac{k}{-5} = -5$ _____

2. $-3 = \frac{n}{7}$ _____

3. $\frac{x}{12} = 0$ _____

4. $-6 = \frac{m}{-2}$ _____

5. $\frac{y}{-4} = -12$ _____

6. $\frac{s}{30} = 6$ _____

7. $\frac{1}{9}z = 0$ _____

8. $-\frac{m}{55} = 1$ _____

9. $-3x = 18$ _____

10. $-56 = 8y$ _____

11. $8p = -8$ _____

12. $-4s = -32$ _____

13. $14h = 42$ _____

14. $-175 = 25g$ _____

15. $-42 = 6m$ _____

16. $-2x = 34$ _____

17. $\frac{x}{-9} = -11$ _____

18. $216 = 9w$ _____

19. $-17v = -17$ _____

20. $-161 = 23t$ _____

21. $56h = 3{,}136$ _____

22. $20 = \frac{e}{-25}$ _____

23. $4{,}200 = 30x$ _____

24. $\frac{y}{-21} = -21$ _____

25. $\frac{m}{-3} = 21$ _____

26. $4{,}000 = \frac{x}{-40}$ _____

27. A bamboo tree grew 3 in. per day. Write and solve an equation to find how many days d it took the tree to grow 144 in.

   Equation: _____ Solution: _____

28. Carl drove 561 miles. His car averages 33 miles per gallon of gas. Write and solve an equation to find how much gas g Carl's car used.

   Equation: _____ Solution: _____

For what values of y is each equation true?

29. $-5|y| = -25$ 30. $\frac{|y|}{2} = 28$ 31. $9|y| = 27$

_____   _____   _____

Name _____ Class _____ Date _____

Reteaching 2-7 Try, Test, Revise

On vacation, your family spent 4 hours driving 220 miles across a state. Part of the time you drove on a scenic state highway at 40 miles per hour. The rest of the time you drove on an interstate at 60 miles per hour. How long did you drive on each type of highway?

Try 3 hours on the state highway. That leaves 1 hour on the interstate. In 3 hours, at 40 miles per hour, you travel 120 miles. In 1 hour, at 60 miles per hour, you drive 60 miles. That is a total of 180 miles, which is not enough. You must have spent more time on the interstate.

Organize the conjectures in a table.

Hours on State Hwy	Hours on Interstate	Distance on State Hwy	Distance on Interstate	Total Distance
3	1	$3(40) = 120$	$1(60) = 60$	$120 + 60 = 180$
2	2	$2(40) = 80$	$2(60) = 120$	$80 + 120 = 200$
1	3	$1(40) = 40$	$3(60) = 180$	$40 + 180 = 220$

Your family traveled one hour on the state highway and three hours on the interstate highway.

Solve using the try, test, revise strategy. Organize your guesses in the table.

1. The Wolverines scored 42 points in a football game. They scored 2 more field goals (3 points each) than touchdowns (6 points each). How many field goals and touchdowns did they score?

Touchdowns	Field Goals	Points From Touchdowns	Points From Field Goals	Total Points

Practice 2-7 Try, Test, Revise

Use the try, test, revise strategy to solve each problem.

1. The length of a rectangle is 9 in. greater than the width. The area is 36 in.^{2} Find the dimensions. _____

Width						
Length						
Area						

2. Shari Williams, a basketball player, scored 30 points on 2-point and 3-point goals. She hit 5 more 2-pointers than 3-pointers. How many of each did she score? _____

3-Pointers						
2-Pointers						
Points						

3. The sums and products of pairs of integers are given. Find each pair of integers.

   a. sum = −12, product = 36 _____

   b. sum = −12, product = 35 _____

   c. sum = −12, product = 32 _____

   d. sum = −12, product = 11 _____

   e. sum = −12, product = 0 _____

4. Jess had 3 more nickels than dimes for a total of $1.50. How many of each coin did he have?

   _____

5. A brush cost $2 more than a comb. The brush and a comb together cost $3.78. Find the cost of each.

   _____

6. The hard-cover edition of a book cost 3 times as much as the paperback edition. Both editions together cost $26.60. Find the cost of each.

   _____

Reteaching 2-8 Inequalities and Their Graphs

Write an inequality for each graph.

a. [number line from −5 to 5, open dot at 2, shaded to the left]

The open dot indicates 2 is not a solution. However, every number less than 2 is a solution. Thus, $x < 2$. Check by testing a point. Since 1 is shaded, try it. Is $1 < 2$? Yes.

b. [number line from −5 to 5, closed dot at −1, shaded to the right]

The closed dot indicates −1 is a solution. Every number greater than −1 is also a solution. Thus, $x \geq -1$. Check by testing a point. Since 2 is shaded, try it. Is $2 \geq -1$? Yes.

Write an inequality for each graph.

1. [number line from −5 to 5, closed dot at −2, shaded to the right]

_____

2. [number line from −5 to 5, closed dot at −3, shaded to the left]

_____

3. [number line from −2 to 8, open dot at 6, shaded to the left]

_____

4. [number line from −5 to 5, open dot at −5, shaded to the right]

_____

5. [number line from −5 to 5, closed dot at 4, shaded to the right]

_____

6. [number line from −5 to 5, open dot at 0, shaded to the right]

_____

7. [number line from −5 to 5, open dot at −1, shaded to the right]

_____

8. [number line from −5 to 5, closed dot at 2, shaded to the right]

_____

9. [number line from −5 to 5, open dot at 3, shaded to the right]

_____

10. [number line from −5 to 5, closed dot at 0, shaded to the left]

_____

Name _____ Class _____ Date _____

Practice 2-8 Inequalities and Their Graphs

Write an inequality for each sentence.

1. The total t is less than sixteen. _____

2. A number h is not less than 7. _____

3. The price p is less than or equal to $25. _____

4. A number n is negative. _____

Write an inequality for each graph.

5.
_____

6.
_____

7.
_____

8.
_____

Graph the solutions of each inequality on a number line.

9. $x < -2$

10. $y \geq -1$

11. $k > 1$

12. $p \leq 4$

Write an inequality for each situation.

13. Everyone in the class is under 13 years old. Let x be the age of a person in the class.

_____

14. The speed limit is 60 miles per hour. Let s be the speed of a car driving within the limit.

_____

15. You have $4.50 to spend on lunch. Let c be the cost of your lunch.

_____

Reteaching 2-9 Solving One-Step Inequalities by Adding or Subtracting

Write an inequality for the sentence. Then solve the inequality. The sum of a number n and seven is greater than twelve.

Words   Sum of a number n and seven is greater than twelve

Inequality n +   7   >   12

To solve, subtract 7 from each side.

$$n + 7 > 12$$
$$n + 7 - 7 > 12 - 7$$
$$n > 5$$

Check: $6 > 5$

Is $6 + 7 > 12$? Yes.

Write an inequality for each sentence. Then solve the inequality.

1. Eight less than a number k is less than 5.

   _____

2. Nine plus a number x is greater than or equal to negative two.

   _____

3. Five subtracted from a number p is less than or equal to negative ten.

   _____

4. A number d plus 17 is less than 25.

   _____

5. The sum of a number s and six is greater than negative seven.

   _____

6. Ten subtracted from a number y is less than twenty.

   _____

7. 82 plus a number j is greater than or equal to -28.

   _____

8. A number n minus 9 is less than or equal to -23.

   _____

9. Nineteen less than a number h is greater than three.

   _____

Practice 2-9 Solving One-Step Inequalities by Adding or Subtracting

Write an inequality for each sentence. Then solve the inequality.

1. Six less than n is less than -4.

_____

2. The sum of a number k and five is greater than or equal to two.

_____

3. Nine more than a number b is greater than negative three.

_____

4. You must be at least 48 inches tall to ride an amusement park ride, and your little sister is 39 inches tall. How many inches i must she grow before she may ride the ride?

_____

5. You need no more than 3,000 calories in a day. You consumed 840 calories at breakfast and 1,150 calories at lunch. How many calories c can you eat for dinner?

_____

Solve each inequality. Graph the solutions.

6. $7 + x \geq 9$ _____

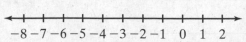

7. $-5 \leq x - 6$ _____

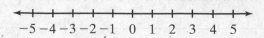

8. $0 \geq x + 12$ _____

-16   -12   -8   -4   0   4

9. $x - 15 \leq -8$ _____

-2 -1 0 1 2 3 4 5 6 7 8

10. $13 + x \geq 13$ _____

-5 -4 -3 -2 -1 0 1 2 3 4 5

11. $x - 8 > -5$ _____

-5 -4 -3 -2 -1 0 1 2 3 4 5

12. $4 + x < -2$ _____

-8 -7 -6 -5 -4 -3 -2 -1 0 1 2

13. $x - 9 > -11$ _____

-5 -4 -3 -2 -1 0 1 2 3 4 5

14. $x - 6 \leq -1$ _____

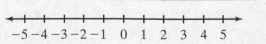

15. $-4 + x < -4$ _____

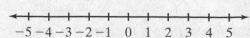

Reteaching 2-10 Solving One-Step Inequalities by Multiplying or Dividing

Solve $5x < -40$.

$5x < -40$

Since 5 and x are multiplied, use a division property of inequality and divide each side by 5.

$5x < -40$

$\frac{5x}{5} < \frac{-40}{5}$

$x < -8$

Solve $\frac{x}{-4} \geq 3$.

Since x is divided by -4, use a multiplication property of inequality and multiply each side by -4.

When you multiply each side of an inequality by a negative number, you must reverse the direction of the inequality symbol.

$\frac{x}{-4} \geq 3$

$(-4)\frac{x}{-4} \leq (-4)3$

$x \leq -12$

Solve each inequality.

1. $7n \geq 42$

_____

2. $-3m < 27$

_____

3. $\frac{x}{3} > 7$

_____

4. $\frac{y}{4} \leq 8$

_____

5. $\frac{q}{-2} < 5$

_____

6. $-n \geq 2$

_____

7. $27 \leq 3k$

_____

8. $6 \geq \frac{d}{7}$

_____

9. $\frac{r}{-9} < 12$

_____

10. $-13 < \frac{h}{-3}$

_____

11. $-15 \geq -3z$

_____

12. $2f \leq -27$

_____

Practice 2-10 Solving One-Step Inequalities by Multiplying or Dividing

Write an inequality for each sentence. Then solve the inequality.

1. The product of k and -5 is no more than 30.

_____

2. Half of p is at least -7.

_____

3. The product of k and 9 is no more than 18.

_____

4. One-third of p is at least -17.

_____

5. The opposite of g is at least -5.

_____

Solve each inequality.

6. $-5x < 10$ _____

7. $\frac{x}{4} > 1$ _____

8. $-8 < -8x$ _____

9. $\frac{1}{3}x > -2$ _____

10. $48 \geq -12x$ _____

11. $\frac{1}{3}x < -6$ _____

12. $\frac{x}{5} < -4$ _____

13. $-x \leq 2$ _____

Determine whether each number is a solution of $7 \geq -3k$.

14. 2 _____

15. -2 _____

16. 0 _____

17. -3 _____

Justify each step.

18. $-5n \geq 45$

$\dfrac{-5n}{-5} \leq \dfrac{45}{-5}$ _____

$n \leq -9$ _____

Reteaching 3-1 Rounding and Estimating

Estimate $3.85 + $2.79 + $3.06 by three methods.

Round all numbers to the same place value.

Estimate

$3.85   ≈ $4
$2.79   ≈ $3
$3.06   ≈ $3
               $10

Use front-end estimation.

$3.85   →   .9
$2.79   →   .8   Estimate by rounding
$3.06   →   .1
$8   +   1.8 = $9.80

Use clustering.

The values cluster around $3. → 3 · 3 = $9

Estimate by rounding each number in an exercise to the same place value.

1.   5.743 ≈
     + 8.216 ≈ _____

2.   73.85 ≈
     − 27.41 ≈ _____

Estimate using front-end estimation.

3.   7.532 ≈
     + 4.859 ≈ _____
          + ____ = _____

4.   26.52 ≈
     + 38.46 ≈ _____
          + ____ = _____

5.   11.2 ≈
     + 16.7 ≈ _____
          + ____ = _____

6.   0.153 ≈
     + 0.479 ≈ _____
          + ____ = _____

Estimate by clustering.

7. $9.85 + $10.26 + $9.07 + 11.01 _____

8. $48.02 + $53.17 + $46.89 _____

9. 121.7 + 112.6 + 130.2 _____

10. 6.3 + 5.9 + 8.2 + 7.1 + 7.7 _____

Practice 3-1 Rounding and Estimating

Estimate using front-end estimation.

1. 6.3 + 8.55

_____

2. 345 + 682

_____

3. 4.60 + 5.53

_____

4. $6.14 + $9.38

_____

5. $39.65 + $25.84

_____

6. 9.71 + 3.94

_____

Estimate by clustering.

7. $7.04 + $5.95 + $6.08 + $5.06 + $6.12

_____

8. 9.3 + 8.7 + 8.91 + 9.052

_____

9. 37.6 + 44.91 + 41 + 39.1

_____

10. 2.357 + 1.874 + 1.956

_____

Estimate by rounding each number to the same place value.

11. 14.66 + 25.19 _____

12. 8.7 + 3.21 + 3.899 _____

13. 194.78 − 12.31 _____

14. $289 − $67.20 _____

15. 800 − 301.47 _____

16. 0.06 + 19.41 _____

Round to the underlined place value.

17. 6.739 _____

18. 52.192 _____

19. 0.61 _____

20. 348.508 _____

Estimate. State your method (rounding, front-end, or clustering).

21. 91.7 + 88.6 + 89.1 + 92.5 + 90.6 _____

22. 3.9 + 8.1 + 2.06 _____

23. $1.08 + $.95 + $.89 + $1.14 _____

24. 11.56 + 19.43 + 13.40 + 14.39 _____

25. 0.015 + 0.039 + 0.0266 _____

Reteaching 3-2 *Estimating Decimal Products and Quotients*

Estimate $3.14 ÷ $0.75.

Round 0.75. Since 5 is 5 or greater, add one to the 7, so 0.75 ≈ 0.8.

Round 3.14 to a compatible number, one that is easy to divide by 0.8. Since 8 · 4 = 32, round 3.14 to 3.2.

Mentally divide 3.2 ÷ 0.8 = 4.

Thus $3.14 ÷ 0.75 ≈ $4.

Estimate each quotient using compatible numbers.

1. 15.831 ÷ 7.87 ≈ _____ ÷ _____ = _____

2. 163.7 ÷ 0.46 ≈ _____ ÷ _____ = _____

3. −472 ÷ 78.6 ≈ _____ ÷ _____ = _____

4. 11.45 ÷ 3.2 ≈ _____ ÷ _____ = _____

5. 549.7 ÷ 51.4 ≈ _____ ÷ _____ = _____

6. −9.6 ÷ (−1.854) ≈ _____ ÷ (_____) = _____

7. 6.39 ÷ (−0.82) ≈ _____ ÷ (_____) = _____

8. −31.8 ÷ 0.56 ≈ _____ ÷ _____ = _____

9. 336.4 ÷ (−4.23) ≈ _____ ÷ (_____) = _____

10. 82.56 ÷ 8.72 ≈ _____ ÷ _____ = _____

11. −62.31 ÷ 14.89 ≈ _____ ÷ _____ = _____

12. 25.8 ÷ 6.72 ≈ _____ ÷ _____ = _____

13. 131 ÷ 42.1 ≈ _____ ÷ _____ = _____

14. 1.53 ÷ 0.28 ≈ _____ ÷ _____ = _____

15. 6,243 ÷ (−75) ≈ _____ ÷ (_____) = _____

Practice 3-2 Estimating Decimal Products and Quotients

Determine whether each product or quotient is reasonable. If it is not reasonable, find a reasonable result.

1. $62.77(29.8) = 187.0546$

2. $16.132 \div 2.96 = 54.5$

3. $(47.89)(6.193) = 296.5828$

4. $318.274 \div 4.07 = 78.2$

5. $2.65(-0.84) = -0.2226$

6. $-38.6(-1.89) = 7.2954$

7. $6,355 \div 775 = 8.2$

8. $1,444.14 \div 67.8 = 213$

9. $1.839(6.3) = 115.857$

10. $3.276 \div 0.63 = 5.2$

Estimate each product or quotient.

11. $8.73 \cdot 6.01$ _____

12. $11.042(4.56)$ _____

13. $197.4 \cdot 2.85$ _____

14. $675.1 \cdot 0.051$ _____

15. $479.2(3.2)$ _____

16. $712.9 \cdot 0.41$ _____

17. $11.57 \div 3.09$ _____

18. $43.68 \div 8.7$ _____

19. $29.5 \div 5.1$ _____

20. $\$41.09 \div \$6.88$ _____

21. $148.8 \div 9.8$ _____

22. $\$76.77 \div \$24.19$ _____

23. Apples cost $.89 per lb. Estimate the cost of three 5-lb bags. _____

24. You buy 3 dinners that are $6.85 each. Before tax and tip, the total is $25.42. Is this total correct? Explain.

25. You worked 18 hours last week and received $92.70 in your paycheck. Estimate your hourly pay.

Reteaching 3-3 Mean, Median, and Mode

In 1995, eight states had pupil-teacher ratios that were close to the U.S. average of 17.3. Use the table at the right. Find the **a)** mean, **b)** median, and **c)** mode.

State	Pupils per Teacher
Arkansas	17.1
Illinois	17.1
Indiana	17.5
Louisiana	17.0
Mississippi	17.5
New Mexico	17.0
Ohio	17.1
Pennsylvania	17.0

a. Mean: $\frac{\text{sum of data items}}{\text{number of data items}}$

$= \frac{17.1 + 17.1 + 17.5 + 17.0 + 17.5 + 17.0 + 17.1 + 17.0}{8}$

$= \frac{137.3}{8} = 17.1625$

Rounded to the nearest tenth, the mean is 17.2.

b. Median: Write the data in order.

17.0, 17.0, 17.0, $\boxed{17.1, 17.1,}$ 17.1, 17.5, 17.5

$\frac{17.1 + 17.1}{2} = 17.1$ Find the mean of the two middle numbers. The median is 17.1.

c. Mode: Find the data item that occurs most often.

Both 17.0 and 17.1 occur 3 times. The modes are 17.0 and 17.1.

Find the mean, median, and mode. Round to the nearest tenth where necessary.

	mean	median	mode

1. 14.2 14.7 14.3 14.6 _____ _____ _____

2. 8 7 3 5 9 2 4 7 _____ _____ _____

3. 37 42 51 28 36 _____ _____ _____

4. 1.1 1.8 2.6 1.8 1.9 2.6 _____ _____ _____

The world's largest body of freshwater is formed by the Great Lakes of North America. Use the table of depths at the right. Find the following statistics. Round to the nearest tenth where necessary.

Lake	Depth (in ft)
Superior	1,333
Michigan	923
Huron	750
Erie	210
Ontario	802

5. mean: _____

6. median: _____

7. mode: _____

Practice 3-3 Mean, Median, and Mode

1. There were 8 judges at a gymnastics competition. Kathleen received these scores for her performance on the uneven parallel bars:
   8.9, 8.7, 8.9, 9.2, 8.8, 8.2, 8.9, 8.8

   a. Find these statistics: mean _____ median _____ mode _____

   b. Which measure of central tendency best describes the data? Explain.

   _____

   _____

   _____

   c. Why do you think that the highest and lowest judge's scores are disregarded in tallying the total score in a gymnastics competition?

   _____

   _____

Find the mean, median, and mode. Round to the nearest tenth where necessary. Identify any outliers.

Data	Mean	Median	Mode	Outliers
2. 8, 15, 9, 7, 4, 5, 9, 11	_____	_____	_____	_____
3. 70, 61, 28, 40, 60, 72, 25, 31, 64, 63	_____	_____	_____	_____
4. 4.9, 5.7, 6.0, 5.3, 4.8, 4.9, 5.3, 4.7, 4.9, 5.6, 5.1	_____	_____	_____	_____
5. 271, 221, 234, 240, 271, 234, 213, 253, 155	_____	_____	_____	_____
6. 0, 2, 3, 3, 3, 4, 4, 5	_____	_____	_____	_____

Use the data in the table. Round to the nearest tenth where necessary.

7. What is the mean height of the five highest European mountains? _____

8. What is the median height? _____

9. Is any of the heights an outlier? Explain.

_____

Peak	Height (ft)
Mont Blanc	15,771
Monte Rosa	15,203
Dom	14,911
Liskamm	14,852
Weisshorn	14,780

Reteaching 3-4 Using Formulas

Given that C is the temperature in degrees Celsius, use the formula
$F = 1.8C + 32$ to find the temperature F in degrees Fahrenheit. What is the
temperature in degrees Fahrenheit for a temperature of 18° in Celsius?

$F = 1.8C + 32$	Write the formula.
$F = 1.8(18) + 32$	Substitute 18 for C.
$F = 32.4 + 32$	Simplify.
$F = 64.4°$	

The temperature is 64.4° Fahrenheit, or 64.4°F.

Find the temperature in degrees Fahrenheit for each temperature in degrees Celsius.

1. $C = 4°$ $F = 1.8($ _____ $) + 32 =$ _____ $+ 32 =$ _____

2. $C = 40°$ $F = 1.8($ _____ $) + 32 =$ _____ $+ 32 =$ _____

3. $C = 22°$ $F = 1.8($ _____ $) + 32 =$ _____ $+ 32 =$ _____

4. $C = 35°$ $F = 1.8($ _____ $) + 32 =$ _____ $+ 32 =$ _____

5. $C = -6°$ $F = 1.8($ _____ $) + 32 =$ _____ $+ 32 =$ _____

6. $C = -24°$ $F = 1.8($ _____ $) + 32 =$ _____ $+ 32 =$ _____

**Given that F is the temperature in degrees Fahrenheit, the formula
$C = (F - 32) \div 1.8$ is the temperature C in degrees Celsius. Find the
temperature in degrees Celsius for each temperature in degrees
Fahrenheit.**

7. $F = 68°$ $C = ($ _____ $- 32) \div 1.8 =$ _____ $\div 1.8 =$ _____

8. $F = 17.6°$ $C = ($ _____ $- 32) \div 1.8 =$ _____ $\div 1.8 =$ _____

9. $F = 5°$ $C = ($ _____ $- 32) \div 1.8 =$ _____ $\div 1.8 =$ _____

10. $F = 57.2°$ $C = ($ _____ $- 32) \div 1.8 =$ _____ $\div 1.8 =$ _____

11. $F = 32°$ $C = ($ _____ $- 32) \div 1.8 =$ _____ $\div 1.8 =$ _____

12. $F = 212°$ $C = ($ _____ $- 32) \div 1.8 =$ _____ $\div 1.8 =$ _____

Name _____ Class _____ Date _____

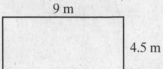

Practice 3-4 Using Formulas

Use the formula $P = 2l + 2w$. Find the perimeter of each rectangle.

1. _____

9 m

4.5 m

2. _____

5.2 ft

1.3 ft

3. _____

12.9 cm

4.7 cm

Use the formula $A = lw$. Find the area of each rectangle above.

4. _____

5. _____

6. _____

7. Use the formula $d = rt$ to find how far each animal in the table can travel in 5 seconds.

Animal	Speed (ft/s)	Distance in 5 s (ft)
Pronghorn antelope	89.5	
Wildebeest	73.3	
Gray fox	61.6	
Wart hog	44.0	
Wild turkey	22.0	
Chicken	13.2	

8. While vacationing on the Mediterranean Sea, Angie recorded the temperature several times during a 24-hour period. She used a thermometer in the lobby of her hotel. It was a beautiful day. Use the formula $F = 1.8C + 32$ to change the temperatures Angie recorded from Celsius to Fahrenheit.

Time	Temperature (°C)	Temperature (°F)
4:00 A.M.	19	
8:00 A.M.	22	
12:00 P.M.	30	
4:00 P.M.	28	
8:00 P.M.	24	
12:00 A.M.	20	

Pre-Algebra Chapter 3

Reteaching 3-5 Solving Equations by Adding or Subtracting Decimals

Solve the equation $n + 3.2 = -4.7$.

$$n + 3.2 = -4.7$$
$$n + 3.2 - 3.2 = -4.7 - 3.2 \quad \text{Subtract 3.2 from each side.}$$
$$n = -7.9 \quad \text{Simplify.}$$

Solve each equation.

1. $n - 17.9 = -31.05$

2. $h + (-8.5) = -0.6$

$n =$ _____

$h =$ _____

3. $y - 33.4 = 81.9$

4. $t + 18.5 = -41$

$y =$ _____

$t =$ _____

5. $h + 20.4 = -15.7$

6. $p - 1.1 = 4.4$

$h =$ _____

$p =$ _____

7. $a + 106.7 = 62.3$

8. $z - 241.6 = 32.7$

$a =$ _____

$z =$ _____

Practice 3-5 Solving Equations by Adding or Subtracting Decimals

Solve each equation.

1. $3.8 = n - 3.62$

2. $x - 19.7 = -17.48$

3. $12.5 = t - 3.55$

4. $k - 263.48 = -381.09$

5. $9.36 + k = 14.8$

6. $-22 = p + 13.7$

7. $y + 3.85 = 2.46$

8. $-13.8 = h + 15.603$

9. $y - 48.763 = 0$

10. $6.21 = e + (-3.48)$

11. $x + (-0.0025) = 0.0024$

12. $-58.109 = v - 47.736$

13. $x + 82.7 = 63.5$

14. $-0.08 = f + 0.07$

15. $0 = a + 27.98$

16. $117.345 + m = 200$

17. $z - 81.6 = -81.6$

18. $5.4 = t + (-6.1)$

19. $-4.095 + b = 18.665$

20. $4.87 = n + 0.87$

Use mental math to solve each equation.

21. $k + 23.7 = 23.7$

22. $5.63 = n + 1.63$

23. $x - 3.2 = 4.1$

24. $p - 0.7 = 9.3$

25. $6.75 + c = 12.95$

26. $-1.09 = j - 4.99$

Reteaching 3-6 Solving Equations by Multiplying or Dividing Decimals

Solve the equations $0.7x = -2.8$ and $\frac{x}{1.5} = 0.2$.

$0.7x = -2.8$	Write the equation.
$\frac{0.7x}{0.7} = \frac{-2.8}{0.7}$	Divide each side by 0.7.
$x = -4$	Simplify.

$\frac{x}{1.5} = 0.2$	Write the equation.
$\frac{x}{1.5}(1.5) = 0.2(1.5)$	Multiply each side by 1.5.
$x = 0.3$	Simplify.

Solve each equation.

1. $4x = -2.44$

2. $1.8x = 5.76$

$x =$ _____

$x =$ _____

3. $\frac{h}{-1.05} = -0.36$

4. $\frac{z}{-0.02} = 5.9$

$h =$ _____

$z =$ _____

5. $4.25y = 0.85$

6. $\frac{n}{-1.9} = 24.6$

$y =$ _____

$n =$ _____

7. $\frac{r}{8.04} = 1.55$

8. $11.32a = -39.62$

$r =$ _____

$a =$ _____

Practice 3-6 Solving Equations by Multiplying or Dividing Decimals

Use mental math to solve each equation.

1. $0.7h = 4.2$ _____

2. $\frac{x}{2.5} = -3$ _____

3. $38.7 = -100k$ _____

4. $-45.6e = -4.56$ _____

Solve each equation.

5. $\frac{p}{2.9} = 0.55$ _____

6. $9.1 = \frac{x}{-0.7}$ _____

7. $-6.4 = \frac{y}{8.5}$ _____

8. $\frac{k}{-1.2} = -0.07$ _____

9. $277.4 = \frac{n}{3.5}$ _____

10. $\frac{e}{-0.76} = 2,809$ _____

11. $\frac{a}{27} = -32.3$ _____

12. $\frac{p}{-1.52} = -3,600$ _____

13. $-9k = 2.34$ _____

14. $-12.42 = 0.03p$ _____

15. $-7.2y = 61.2$ _____

16. $-0.1035 = 0.23n$ _____

17. $1.5m = 3.03$ _____

18. $-0.007h = 0.2002$ _____

19. $8.13t = -100.812$ _____

20. $0.546 = 0.42y$ _____

Write an equation for each sentence. Solve for the variable.

21. The opposite of seventy-five hundredths times some number n equals twenty-four thousandths. Find the value of n.

    _____

22. A number n divided by -3.88 equals negative two thousand. Find the value of n.

    _____

23. Four hundredths times some number n equals thirty-three and four tenths. Find the value of n.

    _____

24. The product of some number n and -0.26 equals 169.39. Find the value of n.

    _____

◼ Reteaching 3-7 *Using the Metric System*

Complete each statement.

a. 2.5 cm = _____ mm
The diagram shows

2.5 cm = ___25___ mm.
You know 10 mm = 1 cm.
Since a mm is smaller, it takes more of them to
make the same length. This can help you
remember to *multiply* by 10.

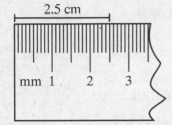

b. 347 g = _____ kg
You know 1,000 g = 1 kg.
A kilogram is heavier than a gram, so it takes fewer to equal the same
weight as 347 g. Thus, divide by 1,000 by moving the decimal point 3
places to the left.

347 g = ___0.347___ kg

Complete each statement.

1. _____ mL = 6.9 L

2. 5.62 cm = _____ mm

3. 5,346 m = _____ km

4. 246 mg = _____ g

5. 890 cm = _____ m

6. 473 cm = _____ mm

7. 9.4 L = _____ mL

8. 29 cg = _____ g

9. 2.1 km = _____ m

10. 1.65 L = _____ cL

11. 37 L = _____ mL

12. 87.5 g = _____ kg

13. 797 mm = _____ m

14. 1.75 km = _____ cm

15. 3,926 mg = _____ g

16. 0.71 kL = _____ L

17. 9,836 cm = _____ km

18. 17.9 g = _____ mg

Practice 3-7 Using the Metric System

Write the metric unit that makes each statement true.

1. 7.84 cm = 78.4 _____

2. 423 m = 0.423 _____

3. 2.8 m = 280 _____

4. 6.5 km = 650,000 _____

Complete each statement.

5. 3.4 cm = _____ mm

6. 197.5 cm = _____ m

7. 7 L = _____ mL

8. 5,247 mg = _____ g

9. 87 g = _____ kg

10. 9,246 mL = _____ L

Choose a reasonable estimate. Explain your choice.

11. the amount of water a cup would hold: 250 mL   250 L

_____

12. the mass of a bag of apples: 2 g   2 kg

_____

13. the height of your kitchen table: 68 cm   68 m

_____

Choose an appropriate metric unit. Explain your choice.

14. distance between two cities

_____

15. the mass of a pencil

_____

16. the capacity of an automobile's gas tank

_____

17. One Olympic event is the 1,500-meter run. How many kilometers is this?

_____

18. A fish pond holds 2,500 liters of water. How many kiloliters is this?

_____

■■■■ Reteaching 3-8 *Simplify a Problem*

You have 12 meters of ribbon to cut into half-meter pieces. How many cuts do you need to make?

Simplify the problem. Suppose you only had 3 meters of ribbon. Use a diagram.

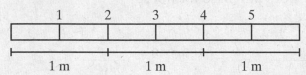

Although you will get 6 pieces of ribbon (2 · 3), you need to make only 5 cuts.

With 12 meters of ribbon, you would get 24 pieces with 23 cuts.

Solve by simplifying the problem.

1. A plumber charges $25 to weld two pipes together. Pipe comes in 4-foot pieces and you need one piece 60 feet long. How much will it cost to have enough 4-foot pieces welded together? Fill in the table first.

Length of Pipe	Number of Welds
8	1
12	2
16	
20	
60	

_____

2. How many digits are used to number the pages of a 425-page book? Fill in the table first.

Page Number	Number of Pages	Digits
1–9		
10–99		
100–425		

Total digits: _____

3. You are serving fruit in small bowls at a luncheon. You decide to place one slice of melon and a spoonful of one type of berry in each bowl. You have three types of melon and four types of berries available. How many different combinations of melon and berries can you make?

_____

Practice 3-8 Simplify a Problem

Solve by simplifying the problem.

1. A house-number manufacturer sold numbers to retail stores for $.09 per digit. A hardware store bought enough digits for two of every house number from 1 to 999. How many digits did the store purchase for house numbers:

   a. 1–9 _____ **b.** 10–99 _____ **c.** 100–999 _____

   d. Find the total cost of the house numbers. _____

2. A tic-tac-toe diagram uses 2 vertical lines and 2 horizontal lines to create 9 spaces. How many spaces can you create using:

   a. 1 vertical line and 1 horizontal line _____

   b. 2 vertical lines and 1 horizontal line _____

   c. 3 vertical lines and 3 horizontal lines _____

   d. 4 vertical lines and 5 horizontal lines _____

   e. 17 vertical lines and 29 horizontal lines _____

3. Each side of each triangle in the figure has length 1 cm. The perimeter (the distance around) the first triangle is 3 cm. Find the perimeter of the figure formed by connecting:

   a. 2 triangles _____ **b.** 3 triangles _____

   c. 4 triangles _____ **d.** 50 triangles _____

Solve using any strategy.

4. At the inauguration, the President was honored with a 21-gun salute. The report from each gunshot lasted 1 s. Four seconds elapsed between shots. How long did the salute last?

   _____

5. Bernie began building a model airplane on day 7 of his summer vacation and finished building it on day 65. He worked on the plane each day. How many days did it take?

   _____

Reteaching 4-1 Divisibility and Factors

Find all the factors of 30.

Start with 1 and 30.
Is 30 divisible by 2? Yes, it ends in 0.
List 2 and 15.

Is 30 divisible by 3? Yes, the sum of the digits, 3, is divisible by 3.
List 3 and 10.

Is 30 divisible by 4? No, $4 \cdot 7 = 28$ and $4 \cdot 8 = 32$.

Is 30 divisible by 5? Yes, it ends in 0.
List 5 and 6.

When you list all the factors in order, the pairs with products of 30 form a symmetric pattern.

1, 2, 3, 5, 6, 10, 15, 30

Fill in the boxes to find all the factors for each number.

1. 34

1, 2, ☐ , 34

2. 50

1, 2, 5, ☐ , ☐ , 50

3. 52

1, ☐ , ☐ , 13, 26, 52

4. 36

1, ☐ , 3, ☐ , 6, 9, ☐ , 18, 36

Find all the factors of each number.

5. 55 _____

6. 40 _____

7. 42 _____

8. 48 _____

Practice 4-1 Divisibility and Factors

List all the factors of each number.

1. 12 _____

2. 45 _____

3. 41 _____

4. 54 _____

5. 48 _____

6. 100 _____

7. 117 _____

Test whether each number is divisible by 2, 3, 5, 9, and 10.

8. 215 _____   **9.** 432 _____

10. 770 _____   **11.** 1,011 _____

12 975 _____   **13.** 2,070 _____

14. 3,707 _____   **15.** 5,715 _____

Write the missing digit to make each number divisible by 9.

16. 7☐1   **17.** 2,2☐2   **18.** 88,☐12

19. There are four different digits which, when inserted in the blank space in the number 4☐5, make the number divisible by 3. Write them.

_____

20. There are two different digits which, when inserted in the blank space in the number 7,16☐, make the number divisible by 5. Write them.

_____

21. There are five different digits which, when inserted in the blank space in the number 99,99☐, make the number divisible by 2. Write them.

_____

Reteaching 4-2 Exponents

Evaluate $(-x)^2$, $-x^2$, and $2(x-4)^2 + 1$ when $x = 9$.

Substitute 9 for x in $(-x)^2$.
$(-9)^2 = (-9)(-9) = 81$

Substitute 9 for x in $-x^2$.
$-9^2 = -(9 \cdot 9) = -81$

Substitute 9 for x in $2(x-4)^2 + 1$.

$$\begin{aligned}
2(x-4)^2 + 1 &= 2(9-4)^2 + 1 & &\text{Substitute 9 for } x. \\
&= 2(5)^2 + 1 & &\text{Work within parentheses first.} \\
&= 2(25) + 1 & &\text{Simplify } (5)^2. \\
&= 50 + 1 & &\text{Multiply.} \\
&= 51 & &\text{Add.}
\end{aligned}$$

Evaluate each expression.

1. $(-a)^2$, for $a = 10$ $(-\underline{\qquad})^2 = \underline{\qquad}$

2. $-a^2$, for $a = 10$ $-\underline{\qquad}^2 = \underline{\qquad}$

3. a^2, for $a = -10$ $(\underline{\qquad})^2 = \underline{\qquad}$

4. $-a^2$, for $a = -10$ $-(\underline{\qquad})^2 = \underline{\qquad}$

5. $-3m^2$, for $m = 5$ $-3(\underline{\qquad})^2 = -3(\underline{\qquad}) = \underline{\qquad}$

6. $2n^2 - 4$, for $n = 3$ $2(\underline{\qquad})^2 - 4 = 2(\underline{\qquad}) - 4$

$= (\underline{\qquad}) - 4 = \underline{\qquad}$

7. $5(2h-4)^2$, for $h = 4$ $5(2 \cdot \underline{\qquad} - 4)^2 = 5(\underline{\qquad} - 4)^2$

$= 5(\underline{\qquad})^2 = 5(\underline{\qquad}) = \underline{\qquad}$

8. xy^2, for $x = 7, y = 2$ $(\underline{\qquad})(\underline{\qquad})^2 = (\underline{\qquad})(\underline{\qquad})$

$= \underline{\qquad}$

Practice 4-2 Exponents

Evaluate each expression.

1. m^4, for $m = 5$ _____

2. $(5a)^3$, for $a = -1$ _____

3. $-(2p)^2$, for $p = 7$ _____

4. $-n^6$, for $n = 2$ _____

5. b^6, for $b = -1$ _____

6. $(e - 2)^3$, for $e = 11$ _____

7. $(6 + h^2)^2$, for $h = 3$ _____

8. $x^2 + 3x - 7$, for $x = -4$ _____

9. $y^3 - 2y^2 + 3y - 4$, for $y = 5$ _____

Write using exponents.

10. $3 \cdot 3 \cdot 3 \cdot 3$ _____

11. $k \cdot k \cdot k \cdot k \cdot k$ _____

12. $(-9)(-9)(-9)m \cdot m \cdot m$ _____

13. $g \cdot g \cdot g \cdot g \cdot h$ _____

14. $7 \cdot a \cdot a \cdot b \cdot b \cdot b$ _____

15. $-8 \cdot m \cdot n \cdot n \cdot 2 \cdot m \cdot m$ _____

16. $d \cdot (-3) \cdot e \cdot e \cdot d \cdot (-3) \cdot e$ _____

Simplify each expression.

17. $(-2)^3$ and -2^3 _____

18. 0^{12} _____

19. 2^8 and 4^4 _____

20. $-5^2 + 4 \cdot 2^3$ _____

21. $3(8 - 6)^2$ _____

22. $-6^2 + 2 \cdot 3^2$ _____

23. $(-2)(-5)^2(3)$ _____

24. $24 + (11 - 3)^2 \div 4$ _____

25. $(17 - 3)^2 \div (4^2 - 3^2)$ _____

26. $(5 + 10)^2 \div 5^2$ _____

27. $4^3 \div (2^5 - 4^2)$ _____

28. $(-1)^5 \cdot (2^4 - 13)^2$ _____

Reteaching 4-3 Prime Factorization and Greatest Common Factor

Find the GCF of 36 and 54.

$36 = 2^2 \cdot 3^2 = \boxed{2} \cdot 2 \cdot \boxed{3} \cdot 3$ **write the prime**
$54 = 2 \cdot 3^3 = \boxed{2} \cdot 3 \cdot \boxed{3} \cdot 3$ **factorization**

find the common factors

$GCF = 2 \cdot 3 \cdot 3 = 2 \cdot 3^2 = 18$

Notice 2 is the lesser power of 2^2 and 2, and 3^2 is the lesser power of 3^2 and 3^3.

Find the GCF.

1. $50 =$ _____

$35 =$ _____

$GCF =$ _____

2. $75 =$ _____

$30 =$ _____

$GCF =$ _____

3. $48 =$ _____

$60 =$ _____

$GCF =$ _____

4. $45 =$ _____

$72 =$ _____

$GCF =$ _____

5. $98 =$ _____

$42 =$ _____

$GCF =$ _____

6. $24 =$ _____

$80 =$ _____

$GCF =$ _____

7. $315 =$ _____

$360 =$ _____

$GCF =$ _____

8. $156 =$ _____

$208 =$ _____

$GCF =$ _____

Practice 4-3 Prime Factorization and Greatest Common Factor

Find each GCF.

1. 8, 12 _____

2. 36, 54 _____

3. 63, 81 _____

4. 69, 92 _____

5. 15, 28 _____

6. 21, 35 _____

7. 30m, 36n _____

8. 75x^3y^2, 100xy _____

9. 15, 24, 30 _____

10. 48, 80, 128 _____

11. 36hk^3, 60k^2m, 84k^4n _____

12. 2mn , 4m^2n^2 _____

Is each number prime, composite, or neither? For each composite, write the prime factorization.

13. 75 _____

14. 152 _____

15. 432 _____

16. 588 _____

17. 160 _____

18. 108 _____

19. 19 _____

20. 143 _____

21. 531 _____

22. 369 _____

23. 83 _____

24. 137 _____

25. The numbers 3, 5, and 7 are factors of n. Find four other factors of n besides 1.

_____

26. For which expressions is the GCF 8x?

A. 2xy and 4x^2 **B.** 16x^2 and 24xy **C.** 8x^3 and 4x **D.** 24x^2 and 48x^3

▬▬ Reteaching 4-4 Simplifying Fractions

Write $\frac{8ab^2}{12a^2b}$ in simplest form.

$\frac{8ab^2}{12a^2b} = \frac{2 \cdot 2 \cdot 2 \cdot a \cdot b \cdot b}{2 \cdot 2 \cdot 3 \cdot a \cdot a \cdot b}$ Write as a product of prime factors.

$= \frac{\overset{1}{2} \cdot \overset{1}{2} \cdot 2 \cdot \overset{1}{a} \cdot b \cdot \overset{1}{b}}{\underset{1}{2} \cdot \underset{1}{2} \cdot 3 \cdot \underset{1}{a} \cdot a \cdot \underset{1}{b}}$ Divide the numerator and denominator by the common factors.

$= \frac{2b}{3a}$ Remove the common factors.

Write in simplest form.

1. $\frac{8}{22}$ _____

2. $\frac{16}{24}$ _____

3. $\frac{9}{21}$ _____

4. $\frac{20h}{24h}$ _____

5. $\frac{30a^2}{36ab} =$ _____ $=$ _____

6. $\frac{4x^2y}{14xy^2} =$ _____ $=$ _____

7. $\frac{18s^3t^2}{8st^2} =$ _____ $=$ _____

8. $\frac{10pqr}{5p^2q} =$ _____ $=$ _____

9. $\frac{11gh^3}{gh} =$ _____ $=$ _____

10. $\frac{2m^2n}{16m^3n^2} =$ _____ $=$ _____

Practice 4-4 Simplifying Fractions

Write in simplest form.

1. $\frac{10}{15}$ _____

2. $\frac{18}{36}$ _____

3. $\frac{27}{36}$ _____

4. $\frac{12}{15}$ _____

5. $\frac{26}{39}$ _____

6. $\frac{7b}{9b}$ _____

7. $\frac{16y^3}{20y^4}$ _____

8. $\frac{8x}{10y}$ _____

9. $\frac{6xy}{16y}$ _____

10. $\frac{24n^2}{28n}$ _____

11. $\frac{abc}{10abc}$ _____

12. $\frac{30hxy}{54kxy}$ _____

13. $\frac{mn^2}{pm^5n}$ _____

14. $\frac{5jh}{15jh^3}$ _____

15. $\frac{12h^3k}{16h^2k^2}$ _____

16. $\frac{20s^2t^3}{16st^5}$ _____

Find two fractions equivalent to each fraction.

17. $\frac{1}{4}$ _____

18. $\frac{2}{3}$ _____

19. $\frac{3}{5}$ _____

20. $\frac{3}{18}$ _____

21. $\frac{8k}{16k}$ _____

22. $\frac{3m}{8n}$ _____

23. $\frac{5pq}{10p^2q^3}$ _____

24. $\frac{3s^2t^2}{7r}$ _____

25. Monty completed 18 passes in 30 attempts. What fraction of his passes did Monty complete? Write in simplest form.

_____

26. Five new state quarters will be issued by the United States mint this year. What fraction of the states will have quarters issued this year?

_____

Reteaching 4-5 Account for All Possibilities

A taco shop serves beef, chicken, or bean burritos. You can have any burrito on a corn or a flour tortilla and with or without hot sauce. How many different burritos does the shop serve?

The different burritos are listed in the table at the right. To be sure all possibilities are counted, all the beef burritos are listed first. Within those, the two types of beef burritos on a corn tortilla are listed first. The pattern is continued with chicken and then bean burritos.

Filling	Tortilla	Hot Sauce
beef	corn	yes
beef	corn	no
beef	flour	yes
beef	flour	no
chicken	corn	yes
chicken	corn	no
chicken	flour	yes
chicken	flour	no
bean	corn	yes
bean	corn	no
bean	flour	yes
bean	flour	no

Solve each problem by accounting for all possibilities.

1. Kara and Karl love steak, fried chicken, hamburgers, mashed potatoes, and french fries. They like green beans and peas. How many different meals including a meat, potatoes, and a green vegetable can they make from these choices? List all possibilities in the table to find the number of different meals.

   _____

2. You are interested in four different extracurricular activities: jazz band, soccer, debate, and theater. You have time in your schedule for only two activities. How many different combinations of two activities can you pick from the four choices?

   _____

Meat	Potato	Vegetable
steak	mashed	beans
steak	mashed	peas

Practice 4-5 Account for All Possibilities

Solve each problem by accounting for all possibilities.

1. A baseball team has 4 pitchers and 3 catchers. How many different pitcher-catcher combinations are possible? One way to solve this problem is to make a list like the one started below. Finish the list.

   _____

   P1-C1   P2-C1
   P1-C2   P2-C2

   _____   _____

   _____   _____

   _____   _____

   _____   _____

2. The baseball team has 2 first basemen, 3 second basemen, and 2 third basemen. How many combinations of the three positions are possible?

   _____

3. A quarter is tossed 3 times. In how many different orders can heads and tails be tossed?

   _____

4. A quarter is tossed 4 times. In how many different orders can heads and tails be tossed?

   _____

5. Curtains are manufactured in 3 different styles and 5 different colors.

   a. How many different style-color combinations are possible?

   _____

   b. The curtains are produced in 2 different fabrics. How many different style-color-fabric combinations are possible?

   _____

Reteaching 4-6 *Rational Numbers*

Evaluate $\frac{a + 7}{b}$, for $a = 9$ and $b = -2$. Write in simplest form.

$\frac{a + 7}{b} = \frac{9 + 7}{-2}$ Substitute.

     $= \frac{16}{-2}$ Add.

     $= -8$ Write in simplest form.

Evaluate. Write in simplest form.

1. $\frac{a}{b}$, for $a = -12$ and $b = 6$ _____

2. $\frac{m - n}{-4}$, for $m = -5$ and $n = 3$ _____

3. $\frac{2x - 5}{y}$, for $x = 6$ and $y = 21$ _____

4. $\frac{h}{h^2 - 2}$, for $h = 4$ _____

5. $\frac{n}{2m - 8}$, for $m = 2$ and $n = 10$ _____

6. $\frac{x}{3y + 4}$, for $x = 4$ and $y = 6$ _____

7. $\frac{-r - s}{s + 2}$, for $r = -4$ and $s = 2$ _____

8. $\frac{j^2 - k}{k}$, for $j = 4$ and $k = -12$ _____

9. $\frac{10 + f^2}{3f}$, for $f = 6$ _____

10. $\frac{z + 2}{z^2 - 4}$, for $z = 6$ _____

11. $\frac{a^2 + b^2}{2a + b}$, for $a = 4$ and $b = -3$ _____

12. $\frac{e}{f^2 - 2f + 1}$, for $e = -6$ and $f = 5$ _____

13. $\frac{17 - u^2}{v^2 - 4v}$, for $u = -3$ and $v = 2$ _____

14. $\frac{-50}{2x^2 - 3x + 5}$, for $x = -1$ _____

15. $\frac{y^3 - 4y + 6}{y^3}$, for $y = -2$ _____

Practice 4-6 Rational Numbers

Graph the rational numbers below on the same number line.

1. $\frac{3}{4}$

2. $-\frac{1}{4}$

3. -0.5

4. 0.3

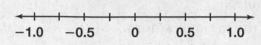

Evaluate. Write in simplest form.

5. $\frac{x}{y}$, for $x = 12$, $y = 21$ _____

6. $\frac{n}{n + p}$, for $n = 9$, $p = 6$ _____

7. $\frac{k}{k^2 + 4}$, for $k = 6$ _____

8. $\frac{x - y}{-21}$, for $x = -2$, $y = 5$ _____

9. $\frac{m}{-n}$, for $m = 6$, $n = 7$ _____

10. $\frac{x(xy - 8)}{60}$, for $x = 3$, $y = 9$ _____

Write three fractions equivalent to each fraction.

11. $\frac{5}{7}$ _____

12. $\frac{22}{33}$ _____

13. $\frac{24}{30}$ _____

14. $\frac{6}{16}$ _____

15. Which of the following rational numbers are equal to $-\frac{17}{10}$?

 $-17, -1.7, -\frac{34}{20}, 0.17$ _____

16. Which of the following rational numbers are equal to $\frac{3}{5}$?

 $\frac{12}{20}, \frac{-3}{-5}, 0.3, \frac{6}{10}$ _____

17. Which of the following rational numbers are equal to $\frac{12}{15}$?

 $\frac{4}{5}, \frac{40}{50}, -\frac{8}{10}, \frac{8}{10}$ _____

18. The weight w of an object in pounds is related to its distance d from the center of Earth by the equation $w = \frac{320}{d^2}$, where d is in thousands of miles. How much does the object weigh at sea level which is about 4,000 miles from the center of Earth?

_____

Reteaching 4-7 *Exponents and Multiplication*

Simplify $m^3 \cdot m^4$ and $(n^2)^3$.

The base of m^3 is m and the base of m^4 is m. So, they have the same base. To multiply variables with the same base, add the exponents.

$m^3 \cdot m^4 = m^{3+4} = m^7$

This rule works because you are combining 3 factors of m and 4 factors of m.

$m^3 \cdot m^4 = (m \cdot m \cdot m) \cdot (m \cdot m \cdot m \cdot m) = m^7$

Simplifying $(n^2)^3$ involves raising a power (n^2) to a power. To find a power of a power, multiply the exponents.

$(n^2)^3 = n^{2 \cdot 3} = n^6$

This rule works because you are using n^2 as a factor 3 times.

$(n^2)^3 = n^2 \cdot n^2 \cdot n^2 = (n \cdot n) \cdot (n \cdot n) \cdot (n \cdot n) = n^6$

Simplify each expression. Show an intermediate step.

1. $4^7 \cdot 4^2 = ($ _____ $) \cdot ($ _____ $) = $ _____

2. $a^3 \cdot a^6 = ($ _____ $) \cdot ($ _____ $) = $ _____

3. $3x^2 \cdot 4x^5 = ($ _____ $) \cdot ($ _____ $) = $ _____

4. $3^4 \cdot 3^3 = ($ _____ $) \cdot ($ _____ $) = $ _____

5. $y^5 \cdot y^3 = ($ _____ $) \cdot ($ _____ $) = $ _____

6. $7r^4 \cdot 3r^2 = ($ _____ $) \cdot ($ _____ $) = $ _____

7. $(5^3)^4 = $ _____ $ = $ _____

8. $(h^2)^5 = $ _____ $ = $ _____

9. $(m^4)^8 = $ _____ $ = $ _____

10. $(x^3 y^2)^3 = $ _____ $ = $ _____

11. $(2s^4 t^5)^4 = $ _____ $ = $ _____

12. $(-pqr^2)^3 = $ _____ $ = $ _____

■ **Practice 4-7** Exponents and Multiplication

Complete each equation.

1. $9^3 \cdot 9^{} = 9^7$

2. $6^8 \cdot 6^{} = 6^{17}$

3. $n^{} \cdot n^5 = n^{15}$

4. $(a^{})^8 = a^{24}$

5. $(c^4)^{} = c^{12}$

6. $r^{} \cdot r^{12} = r^{20}$

Simplify each expression.

7. $(z^3)^5$ _____

8. $-(m^4)^3$ _____

9. $(-3^2)^3$ _____

10. $(x^3)(x^4)$ _____

11. $y^4 \cdot y^5$ _____

12. $(-y^5)(y^2)$ _____

13. $(3y^2)(2y^3)$ _____

14. $3x^{12} \cdot 2x^3$ _____

15. $m^{30} \cdot m^{12}$ _____

16. $(x^4)(y^2)(x^2)$ _____

17. $(-6x^7)(-9x^{12})$ _____

18. $(h^4)^4$ _____

Find the area of each rectangle.

19.

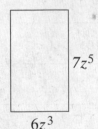

p^2

$3p^4$

20.

$7z^5$

$6z^3$

_____

_____

Compare. Use >, <, or = to complete each statement.

21. $(4^3)^2$ ☐ $(4^2)^3$

22. $5^3 \cdot 5^4$ ☐ 5^{10}

23. $(3^5)^4$ ☐ 3^{10}

24. 3^4 ☐ 9^2

25. $(9^7)^9$ ☐ $(9^8)^8$

26. $4^2 \cdot 4^3$ ☐ 4^5

27. $(6^2)^2$ ☐ $3^4 \cdot 2^4$

28. $5^2 \cdot 5^6$ ☐ 5^7

29. $(8^2)^2$ ☐ $(8^2)^3$

Reteaching 4-8 Exponents and Division

Simplify $\frac{a^3}{a^3}$ and $\frac{m^2}{m^6}$.

To divide variables with the same non-zero base, you subtract the exponents.

$\frac{a^3}{a^3} = a^{3-3}$ Subtract the exponents.

$\quad = a^0$ Simplify the exponent.

However, $\frac{a^3}{a^3} = 1$ as long as a is not zero, just like $\frac{2}{2} = 1, \frac{9}{9} = 1$, and so on.

So $\frac{a^3}{a^3} = 1$ and $a^0 = 1$.

$\frac{m^2}{m^6} = m^{2-6}$ Subtract the exponents.

$\quad = m^{-4}$ Simplify the exponent.

However, $\frac{m^2}{m^6} = \frac{\overset{1}{\cancel{m}} \cdot \overset{1}{\cancel{m}}}{\underset{1}{\cancel{m}} \cdot \underset{1}{\cancel{m}} \cdot m \cdot m \cdot m \cdot m} = \frac{1}{m^4}$

So, $\frac{m^2}{m^6} = \frac{1}{m^4}$ and $m^{-4} = \frac{1}{m^4}$.

The *simplified* form of $\frac{a^3}{a^3}$ is 1, and the *simplified* form of $\frac{m^2}{m^6}$ is $\frac{1}{m^4}$.

Simplify each expression.

1. $\frac{7^8}{7^2}$ _____

2. $\frac{x^5}{x}$ _____

3. 5^0 _____

4. n^{-3} _____

5. $x^{-2}y^4$ _____

6. $6a^{-3}$ _____

7. $(-4)^0$ _____

8. $\frac{b^3}{b^8}$ _____

9. $\frac{y^2}{y^9}$ _____

10. $7s^{-5}t^{-3}$ _____

11. $\frac{3^{18}}{3^3}$ _____

12. $(-729)^0$ _____

13. $\frac{z^7}{z^{34}}$ _____

14. $4e^3f^{-2}$ _____

Practice 4-8 Exponents and Division

Complete each equation.

1. $\frac{8^n}{8^7} = 8^2$, $n =$ _____

2. $\frac{12x^5}{4x} = 3x^n$, $n =$ _____

3. $\frac{1}{h^5} = h^n$, $n =$ _____

4. $\frac{p^n}{p^8} = p^{-6}$, $n =$ _____

5. $\frac{1}{81} = 3^n$, $n =$ _____

6. $\frac{12^4}{12^n} = 1$, $n =$ _____

Simplify each expression.

7. $\frac{a^3}{a^7}$ _____

8. $\frac{j^5}{j^6}$ _____

9. $\frac{x^7}{x^7}$ _____

10. $\frac{k^5}{k^9}$ _____

11. $\frac{9x^8}{12x^5}$ _____

12. $\frac{2f^{10}}{f^5}$ _____

13. $\frac{3y^4}{6y^{-4}}$ _____

14. n^{-5} _____

15. $\frac{3xy^4}{9xy}$ _____

16. $(-15)^0$ _____

17. $\frac{15h^6k^3}{5hk^2}$ _____

18. $4b^{-6}$ _____

Write each expression without a fraction bar.

19. $\frac{a^7}{a^{10}}$ _____

20. $\frac{4x^2y}{2x^3}$ _____

21. $\frac{x^3y^4}{x^9y^2}$ _____

22. $\frac{12mn}{12m^3n^5}$ _____

23. $\frac{16s^2t^4}{8s^5t^3}$ _____

24. $\frac{21e^4f^2}{7e^2}$ _____

25. Write three different quotients that equal 4^{-5}.

_____

Reteaching 4-9 *Scientific Notation*

Write each number in scientific notation, then multiply: $(8,600,000)(0.0042)$.

8.6 is between 1
and 10

$8,600,000. = 8.6 \times 10^6$

6 places
to the left

4.2 is between 1
and 10

$0.0042 = 4.2 \times 10^{-3}$

3 places
to the right

$(8.6 \times 10^6)(4.2 \times 10^{-3}) = 8.6 \times 4.2 \times 10^6 \times 10^{-3}$	Use the commutative property of multiplication.
$= 36.12 \times 10^6 \times 10^{-3}$	Multiply 8.6 and 4.2.
$= 36.12 \times 10^3$	Add the exponents.
$= 3.612 \times 10^1 \times 10^3$	Write 36.12 as 3.612×10^1.
$= 3.612 \times 10^4$	Add the exponents.

Write each number in scientific notation.

1. 745 million _____

2. 0.00034 _____

3. 888,200,000 _____

4. 5,700 _____

Multiply. Write your result using scientific notation.

5. $(1.6 \times 10^6)(3.7 \times 10^4)$ _____

6. $(3 \times 10^{-4})(2 \times 10^{-5})$ _____

7. $72,000 \times 143,000$ _____

8. $(2.3 \times 10^{-2})(1.5 \times 10^4)$ _____

Practice 4-9 Scientific Notation

Write each number in standard notation.

1. 3.77×10^4 _____

2. 8.5×10^3 _____

3. 9.002×10^{-5} _____

4. 1.91×10^{-3} _____

Write each number in scientific notation.

5. Pluto is about 3,653,000,000 mi from the sun. _____

6. There are 63,360 in. in a mile. _____

7. At its closest, Mercury is about 46,000,000 km from the sun. _____

8. 77,250,000 _____

9. 526,000 _____

10. 8 billion _____

11. 8,100,000 _____

12. 0.00000073 _____

13. 0.000903 _____

Multiply. Express each result in scientific notation.

14. $(2 \times 10^5)(3 \times 10^2)$

15. $(1.5 \times 10^5)(4 \times 10^9)$

_____

_____

16. $(6 \times 10^{-4})(1.2 \times 10^{-3})$

17. $(5 \times 10^3)(1.7 \times 10^{-5})$

_____

_____

Order from least to greatest.

18. $72 \times 10^5, 6.9 \times 10^6, 23 \times 10^5$

_____

19. $19 \times 10^{-3}, 2.5 \times 10^{-4}, 1.89 \times 10^{-4}$

_____

20. An ounce is 0.00003125 tons. Write this number in scientific notation.

_____

21. A century is 3,153,600,000 seconds. Write this number in scientific notation.

_____

Reteaching 5-1 Comparing and Ordering Rational Numbers

Compare $\frac{2}{27}$ and $\frac{1}{18}$. Also compare $-\frac{2}{27}$ and $-\frac{1}{18}$.

Step 1: Find the LCM of 27 and 18.

$27 = 3^3$ and $18 = 2 \cdot 3^2$

$LCM = 2 \cdot 3^3 = 54$

Step 2: Write equivalent fractions with a denominator of 54.

$\frac{2 \cdot 2}{27 \cdot 2} = \frac{4}{54}$

$\frac{1 \cdot 3}{18 \cdot 3} = \frac{3}{54}$

Step 3: Compare the fractions.

$4 > 3$, so

$\frac{4}{54} > \frac{3}{54}$ or $\frac{2}{27} > \frac{1}{18}$.

Since $-4 < -3$,

$-\frac{4}{54} < -\frac{3}{54}$ or $-\frac{2}{27} < -\frac{1}{18}$.

Find the LCD of each pair of fractions. Write equivalent fractions using the LCD and compare. Use $>$, $<$, or $=$ to complete each statement.

1. $\frac{2}{9}, \frac{1}{6}$

_____ ☐ _____

2. $\frac{5}{8}, \frac{3}{4}$

_____ ☐ _____

3. $-\frac{2}{3}, -\frac{5}{6}$

_____ ☐ _____

4. $-\frac{5}{18}, -\frac{2}{9}$

_____ ☐ _____

5. $\frac{7}{12}, \frac{11}{18}$

_____ ☐ _____

6. $\frac{13}{20}, \frac{11}{15}$

_____ ☐ _____

7. $-\frac{11}{20}, -\frac{22}{40}$

_____ ☐ _____

8. $\frac{6}{25}, \frac{1}{5}$

_____ ☐ _____

9. $\frac{15}{28}, \frac{4}{7}$

_____ ☐ _____

10. $\frac{5}{9}, \frac{11}{21}$

_____ ☐ _____

11. $\frac{5}{17}, \frac{15}{51}$

_____ ☐ _____

12. $-\frac{5}{12}, -\frac{13}{30}$

_____ ☐ _____

Practice 5-1 Comparing and Ordering Fractions

Compare. Use >, <, or = to complete each statement.

1. $\frac{2}{3} \square \frac{7}{9}$ **2.** $\frac{3}{5} \square \frac{7}{10}$ **3.** $-\frac{3}{4} \square -\frac{13}{16}$

4. $\frac{9}{21} \square \frac{6}{14}$ **5.** $-\frac{2}{8} \square -\frac{7}{32}$ **6.** $\frac{7}{9} \square -\frac{8}{9}$

7. $\frac{5}{8} \square \frac{7}{12}$ **8.** $-\frac{4}{5} \square -\frac{7}{8}$ **9.** $-\frac{4}{18} \square -\frac{6}{27}$

10. $\frac{8}{17} \square -\frac{3}{8}$ **11.** $\frac{4}{7} \square 2\frac{4}{7}$ **12.** $\frac{-9}{-11} \square \frac{9}{11}$

13. $\frac{1}{3} \square -\frac{3}{9}$ **14.** $-\frac{12}{6} \square -\frac{9}{3}$ **15.** $-\frac{5}{10} \square \frac{-3}{-4}$

Find the LCM of each group of numbers or expressions.

16. 7, 21 _____   **17.** 24, 32 _____

18. 15, 50 _____   **19.** $9a^3b, 18abc$ _____

20. $28xy^2, 42x^2y$ _____   **21.** 9, 12, 16 _____

22. A quality control inspector in an egg factory checks every forty-eighth egg for cracks and every fifty-fourth egg for weight. What is the number of the first egg each day that the inspector checks for both qualities?

_____

23. A stock sold for $3\frac{5}{8}$ one day and $3\frac{1}{2}$ the next. Did the value of the stock go up or down? Explain.

_____

24. Marissa needs $2\frac{2}{3}$ yards of ribbon for a wall-hanging she wants to make. She has $2\frac{3}{4}$ yards. Does she have enough ribbon? Explain.

_____

Order from least to greatest.

25. $\frac{2}{3}, \frac{3}{4}, \frac{1}{2}$ **26.** $\frac{2}{5}, \frac{1}{3}, \frac{3}{7}, \frac{4}{9}$ **27.** $\frac{8}{11}, \frac{9}{10}, \frac{7}{8}, \frac{3}{4}$

_____   _____   _____

Reteaching 5-2 *Fractions and Decimals*

Write $1.5\overline{3}$ as a mixed number in simplest form.

$n = 1.533333\ldots$	Let the variable n equal the decimal. Note that the bar is over only the 3, so only the 3 repeats.
$100n = 153.3333\ldots$	Multiply each side by 10^2 or 100 to bring one of the repeating 3's left of the decimal.
$10n = 15.3333\ldots$	Multiply each side by 10 so the repeating 3's will subtract out.
$100n = 153.3333\ldots$ $-\ 10n = -\ 15.3333\ldots$	Subtract to eliminate the repeating 3's.
$90n = 138$	Solve the new equation
$\frac{90n}{90} = \frac{138}{90}$	Divide each side by 90.
$n = 1\frac{48}{90}$	
$n = 1\frac{48\ \div\ 6}{90\ \div\ 6}$	Divide the numerator and denominator by the GCF, 6.
$= 1\frac{8}{15}$	

Write each decimal as a fraction or mixed number in simplest form.

1. $0.\overline{63}$

$n = $ _____

$100n = $ _____

$-\ n = $ _____

$99n = $ _____

$\frac{99n}{99} = $ _____

$n = $ _____

2. $0.8\overline{3}$

$n = $ _____

$100n = $ _____

$-\ 10n = $ _____

$90n = $ _____

$\frac{90n}{90} = $ _____

$n = $ _____

3. $1.7\overline{2}$ _____

4. $0.\overline{57}$ _____

5. $4.\overline{90}$ _____

6. $2.2\overline{6}$ _____

Practice 5-2 Fractions and Decimals

Write as a fraction or mixed number in simplest form.

1. 0.4 _____

2. 0.75 _____

3. 0.16 _____

4. 2.34 _____

5. 0.09 _____

6. 8.8 _____

Write each fraction or mixed number as a decimal.

7. $\frac{17}{20}$ _____

8. $\frac{7}{8}$ _____

9. $-\frac{9}{16}$ _____

10. $3\frac{1}{8}$ _____

11. $6\frac{9}{32}$ _____

12. $2\frac{87}{125}$ _____

13. $\frac{13}{25}$ _____

14. $4\frac{31}{50}$ _____

15. $-\frac{7}{12}$ _____

16. $\frac{4}{9}$ _____

17. $\frac{5}{18}$ _____

18. $\frac{15}{11}$ _____

Order from least to greatest.

19. $0.4, \frac{3}{5}, \frac{1}{2}, \frac{3}{10}$ _____

20. $-\frac{3}{8}, -\frac{3}{4}, -0.38, -0.6$ _____

21. $\frac{1}{4}, -\frac{1}{5}, 0.2, \frac{2}{5}$ _____

22. Write an improper fraction with the greatest possible value using each of the digits 5, 7, and 9 once. Write this as a mixed number and as a decimal.

_____

Write each decimal as a fraction or mixed number in simplest form.

23. $10.0\overline{7}$ _____

24. 3.44 _____

25. $-4.\overline{27}$ _____

26. 0.09 _____

27. 0.375 _____

28. $0.2\overline{43}$ _____

Compare. Use $<$, $>$, or $=$ to complete each statement.

29. $\frac{5}{6}$ ☐ 0.8

30. $\frac{7}{11}$ ☐ 0.65

31. $4.\overline{2}$ ☐ $4\frac{2}{9}$

32. $-\frac{3}{11}$ ☐ -0.25

33. $0.\overline{80}$ ☐ $\frac{80}{99}$

34. -0.43 ☐ $-\frac{7}{16}$

Reteaching 5-3 Adding and Subtracting Fractions

Subtract $3\frac{1}{3} - 1\frac{5}{6}$.

Find a common denominator.

$3\frac{1}{3} = \qquad 3\frac{2}{6} =$

$- 1\frac{5}{6} = \qquad - 1\frac{5}{6} =$

Rename $3\frac{2}{6}$ and subtract.

$2\frac{8}{6}$

$- 1\frac{5}{6}$

$1\frac{3}{6} = 1\frac{1}{2}$ Simplify.

Note: $3\frac{2}{6} = 2 + 1 + \frac{2}{6} = 2 + \frac{6}{6} + \frac{2}{6} = 2 + \frac{8}{6} = 2\frac{8}{6}$

Find each difference.

1. $2\frac{4}{5} = \qquad 2$

$- 1\frac{1}{10} = \quad - 1$

2. $4\frac{2}{3} = \quad 4\frac{\square}{\square} = \quad 3\frac{\square}{\square}$

$- 2\frac{11}{12} = \quad - 2\frac{\square}{\square} = \quad - 2\frac{\square}{\square}$

3. $5\frac{1}{9} = \quad 5\frac{\square}{\square} = 4\frac{\square}{\square}$

$- 2\frac{5}{6} = \quad - 2\frac{\square}{\square} = 2\frac{\square}{\square}$

4. $7\frac{2}{15} = \quad 7\frac{\square}{\square} = \quad 6\frac{\square}{\square}$

$- 1\frac{7}{10} = \quad - 1\frac{\square}{\square} = \quad - 1\frac{\square}{\square}$

5. $3\frac{4}{9} - 2\frac{1}{18}$ _____

6. $6\frac{1}{3} - 2\frac{2}{5}$ _____

7. $7\frac{2}{7} - 3\frac{5}{6}$ _____

8. $2\frac{7}{18} - 1\frac{3}{4}$ _____

9. $10\frac{3}{7} - 5\frac{1}{14}$ _____

10. $1\frac{5}{8} - 1\frac{1}{6}$ _____

11. $2\frac{1}{5} - 1\frac{4}{9}$ _____

12. $11\frac{3}{5} - 9\frac{17}{20}$ _____

13. $5\frac{5}{36} - 4\frac{8}{9}$ _____

14. $3\frac{2}{9} - 3\frac{2}{3}$ _____

Practice 5-3 Adding and Subtracting Fractions

Find each sum or difference.

1. $\frac{2}{3} + \frac{1}{6}$ _____

2. $\frac{5}{8} - \frac{1}{4}$ _____

3. $2 - \frac{5}{7}$ _____

4. $1\frac{1}{2} - 2\frac{4}{5}$ _____

5. $\frac{1}{4} - \frac{1}{3}$ _____

6. $5\frac{7}{8} + 3\frac{5}{12}$ _____

7. $\frac{x}{3} + \frac{x}{5}$ _____

8. $\frac{2n}{5} + \left(-\frac{n}{6}\right)$ _____

9. $\frac{7}{12} - \frac{3}{12}$ _____

10. $3\frac{1}{5} + 2\frac{2}{5}$ _____

11. $1\frac{5}{8} - 1\frac{1}{8}$ _____

12. $\frac{3}{5y} + \frac{1}{5y}$ _____

13. $\frac{9}{16} + \frac{3}{4}$ _____

14. $2\frac{7}{10} - 3\frac{7}{20}$ _____

15. $3\frac{5}{6} + 2\frac{3}{4}$ _____

16. $-1\frac{2}{3} + \left(-2\frac{1}{4}\right)$ _____

Find each sum using mental math.

17. $3\frac{3}{8} + 2\frac{1}{8} + 1\frac{3}{8}$ _____

18. $6\frac{7}{12} + 4\frac{5}{12}$ _____

19. $8\frac{3}{16} + 2\frac{5}{16} + 4\frac{7}{16}$ _____

20. $7\frac{9}{10} + 3\frac{3}{10}$ _____

Estimate each sum or difference.

21. $13\frac{4}{5} - 2\frac{9}{10}$ _____

22. $18\frac{3}{8} + 11\frac{6}{7}$ _____

23. $23\frac{6}{13} + 32\frac{7}{8}$ _____

24. $26\frac{9}{10} + 72\frac{5}{6}$ _____

Use prime factors to simplify each expression.

25. $\frac{7}{30} - \frac{29}{75}$ _____

26. $\frac{3}{14} + \frac{17}{63}$ _____

27. $\frac{5}{42} + \frac{5}{12}$ _____

28. $2\frac{5}{6} - 2\frac{5}{22}$ _____

29. $4\frac{4}{15} + 2\frac{4}{39}$ _____

30. $3\frac{5}{9} - 2\frac{11}{12}$ _____

Reteaching 5-4 Multiplying and Dividing Fractions

Find $3\frac{2}{3} \cdot 1\frac{4}{5}$.

$3\frac{2}{3} \cdot 1\frac{4}{5} = \frac{11}{3} \cdot \frac{9}{5}$ Change to improper fractions.

$= \frac{11}{\overset{}{\underset{1}{3}}} \cdot \frac{\overset{3}{9}}{5}$ Divide the common factors.

$= \frac{33}{5} = 6\frac{3}{5}$ Simplify.

Find $-1\frac{1}{2} \div 2\frac{1}{4}$.

$-1\frac{1}{2} \div 2\frac{1}{4} = -\frac{3}{2} \div \frac{9}{4}$ Change to improper fractions.

$= -\frac{\overset{1}{3}}{\underset{1}{2}} \cdot \frac{\overset{2}{4}}{\underset{3}{9}}$ Multiply by the reciprocal.

$= -\frac{1}{1} \cdot \frac{2}{3}$ Divide the common factors.

$= -\frac{2}{3}$ Simplify.

Check your sign with the original problem. A negative times a positive has a negative product.

Find each product.

1. $\frac{7}{9} \cdot \frac{3}{7} =$ _____

2. $2\frac{1}{5} \cdot \left(-1\frac{1}{11}\right) =$ _____

3. $-3\frac{7}{8} \cdot 2\frac{2}{3} =$ _____

4. $5\frac{1}{7} \cdot 4\frac{2}{3} =$ _____

Find each quotient.

5. $-\frac{6}{11} \div \frac{4}{11} =$ _____

6. $1\frac{1}{6} \div 2\frac{1}{3} =$ _____

7. $-4\frac{1}{5} \div \left(-1\frac{3}{4}\right) =$ _____

8. $-6\frac{1}{8} \div \frac{7}{3} =$ _____

Practice 5-4 Multiplying and Dividing Fractions

Find each quotient.

1. $\frac{1}{2} \div \frac{5}{8}$ _____

2. $-\frac{5}{24} \div \frac{7}{12}$ _____

3. $\frac{3}{8} \div \frac{6}{7}$ _____

4. $\frac{15}{19} \div \frac{15}{19}$ _____

5. $8 \div \frac{4}{5}$ _____

6. $6\frac{1}{4} \div 2\frac{1}{2}$ _____

7. $5\frac{5}{8} \div 1\frac{1}{4}$ _____

8. $2\frac{1}{3} \div \frac{7}{10}$ _____

9. $\frac{6}{35t} \div \frac{3}{7t}$ _____

10. $1\frac{3}{7} \div \left(-2\frac{1}{7}\right)$ _____

Find each product.

11. $\frac{2}{5} \cdot \frac{3}{7}$ _____

12. $\frac{5}{9} \cdot \frac{3}{5}$ _____

13. $\frac{7}{9} \cdot \frac{6}{13}$ _____

14. $\frac{5}{6} \cdot \left(-1\frac{3}{10}\right)$ _____

15. $-4\frac{2}{3}\left(-5\frac{1}{6}\right)$ _____

16. $2\frac{5}{6}\left(-\frac{2}{5}\right)$ _____

17. $4\frac{7}{8} \cdot 6$ _____

18. $\frac{5x}{7} \cdot \frac{3}{10}$ _____

19. $\frac{9a}{10} \cdot \frac{5}{12a}$ _____

20. $\frac{9t}{16} \cdot \frac{12}{17}$ _____

21. You are making cookies for a bake sale. The recipe calls for $2\frac{3}{4}$ cups of flour. How much flour will you need if you triple the recipe?

_____

22. It took you 1 hour to read $1\frac{3}{8}$ chapters of a novel. At this rate, how many chapters can you read in three hours?

_____

23. A teacher wants to tape sheets of paper together to make a science banner. He wants the banner to be $127\frac{1}{2}$ inches long, and each sheet of paper is $8\frac{1}{2}$ inches wide. How many sheets of paper will he need?

_____

Reteaching 5-5 *Using Customary Units of Measurement*

Use dimensional analysis to convert 36 ounces to pounds.

$36 \text{ oz} = \frac{36 \text{ oz}}{1} \cdot \frac{1 \text{ lb}}{16 \text{ oz}}$ Multiply by a fraction that is equal to one and compares pounds to ounces.

$= \frac{\overset{9}{\cancel{36}} \text{ oz} \cdot 1 \text{ lb}}{1 \cdot \underset{4}{\cancel{16}} \text{ oz}}$ Divide the common factors and units.

$= \frac{9}{4} \text{ lb} = 2\frac{1}{4} \text{ lb}$ Simplify.

There are $2\frac{1}{4}$ lb in 36 oz.

Convert from one unit to the other.

1. 12 fl oz = _____ c

2. 42 in = _____ ft

3. 6,600 ft = _____ mi

4. 5,000 lb = _____ t

5. $3\frac{1}{8}$c = _____ fl oz

6. $2\frac{3}{8}$lb = _____ oz

7. 2 gal 2 qt = _____ qt

8. 1 yd 2 ft = _____ ft

9. 2 ton 800 lb = _____ lb

10. 15 qt = _____ gal

11. 23 pt = _____ gal

12. 81 in. = _____ yd

Practice 5-5 Using Customary Units of Measurement

Use estimation, mental math, or paper and pencil to convert from one unit to the other.

1. 2 gal 2 qt = _____ qt

2. 3 yd = _____ ft

3. 1 ft 8 in. = _____ in.

4. $\frac{3}{5}$ t = _____ lb

5. 30 in. = _____ ft

6. 20 fl oz = _____ c

7. 20 oz = _____ lb

8. $2\frac{1}{2}$ pt = _____ c

9. $1\frac{1}{8}$ lb = _____ oz

10. 7920 ft = _____ mi

Is each measurement reasonable? If not, give a reasonable measurement.

11. A glass of milk holds about 8 pt.

_____

12. A newborn baby weighs about $7\frac{1}{2}$ oz.

_____

13. A phonebook is $\frac{3}{4}$ ft wide.

_____

Choose an appropriate unit of measure. Explain your choice.

14. weight of a whale

_____

15. sugar in a cookie recipe

_____

16. length of a mouse

_____

Should each item be measured by *length*, *weight*, or *capacity*?

17. amount of soup in a can

_____

18. height of a can

_____

19. heaviness of a can

_____

20. diameter of a can

_____

Reteaching 5-6 Work Backward

Jody, Karl, and Kara want to buy a pizza. Jody said she can pay half the cost. Karl said he can pay $\frac{1}{3}$ of what was left after Jody paid half. Kara said she could pay the remaining $4. How much does the pizza cost?

Work backward.

Kara will pay $4. This is $\frac{2}{3}$ of what is left after Jody pays half, since Karl pays $\frac{1}{3}$ and $1 - \frac{1}{3} = \frac{2}{3}$. Let h equal half the cost of the pizza.

$\frac{2}{3}h = 4$

Use the Try, Test, Revise strategy to find $h = 6$.

Thus, Jody pays $6 and Karl pays $\frac{1}{3} \cdot 6 = \$2$.

The pizza costs $6 + 2 + 4 = \$12$.

1. Steven, Lisa, and Mark want to buy a pizza. Steven said he could pay twice as much as Lisa. Mark said he could pay the remaining $3, which is $1 less than Lisa's share. How much does the pizza cost?

   a. How much is Mark paying? _____

   b. How much is Lisa paying? _____

   c. How much is Steven paying? _____

   d. How much does the pizza cost? _____

2. On Wednesday, Olga's parents said she owed them too much money to borrow any more. On Thursday, she paid her parents $15 she had earned babysitting. On Friday, she borrowed $5 to go to a movie. On Saturday, she paid them the $12 she earned babysitting. Then her debt was down to $22. How much did she owe on Wednesday?

   _____

3. Yuki, Mollie, Brandon, and Anna share an apple pie for dessert. Brandon eats half the amount Mollie eats. Yuki eats four times as much pie as Brandon. Mollie eats $\frac{1}{4}$ of the pie. How much does Anna eat?

   _____

Practice 5-6 Work Backward

Work backward to solve each problem.

1. Manuel's term paper is due on March 31. He began doing research on March 1. He intends to continue doing research for 3 times as long as he has done already. Then he will spend a week writing the paper and the remaining 3 days typing. What day is it? (Assume he will finish typing on March 30.)

    _____

2. A disc jockey must allow time for 24 minutes of commercials every hour, along with 4 minutes for news, 3 minutes for weather, and 2 minutes for public-service announcements. If each record lasts an average of 3 minutes, how many records per hour can the DJ play?

    _____

3. Margaret is reading the 713-page novel *War and Peace*. When she has read twice as many pages as she has read already, she will be 119 pages from the end. What page is she on now?

    _____

4. On Monday the low temperature at the South Pole dropped 9°F from Sunday's low. On Tuesday it fell another 7°, then rose 13° on Wednesday and 17° more on Thursday. Friday it dropped 8° to −50°F. What was Sunday's low temperature?

    _____

5. Each problem lists the operations performed on n to produce the given result. Find n.
    a. Multiply by 3, add 4, divide by 5, subtract 6; result, −1.

    $n =$ _____

    b. Add 2, divide by 3, subtract 4, multiply by 5; result, 35.

    $n =$ _____

    c. Multiply by 2, add 7, divide by 17; result, 1.

    $n =$ _____

    d. Divide by 3, add 9, multiply by 2, subtract 12; result, 4.

    $n =$ _____

    e. Subtract 2, divide by 5, add 7, multiply by 3; result, 30.

    $n =$ _____

Reteaching 5-7 Solving Equations by Adding or Subtracting Fractions

Solve $h - 2\frac{3}{4} = -3\frac{1}{6}$.

$$h - 2\frac{3}{4} = -3\frac{1}{6}$$

$h - 2\frac{3}{4} + 2\frac{3}{4} = -3\frac{1}{6} + 2\frac{3}{4}$ Add $2\frac{3}{4}$ to each side.

$h = -3\frac{2}{12} + 2\frac{9}{12}$ Use a common denominator.

$h = -2\frac{14}{12} + 2\frac{9}{12}$ Rename $-3\frac{2}{12}$ as $-2\frac{14}{12}$.

$h = -\frac{5}{12}$ Subtract $2\frac{14}{12} - 2\frac{9}{12}$. The sum is negative because $\left|-3\frac{1}{6}\right| > \left|2\frac{3}{4}\right|$.

Solve each equation.

1. $h + \frac{3}{4} = \frac{7}{8}$ _____

2. $e + 1\frac{13}{16} = 2\frac{5}{16}$ _____

3. $m + \frac{5}{8} = -\frac{3}{16}$ _____

4. $p - 4\frac{5}{12} = 2\frac{7}{12}$ _____

5. $x - \frac{5}{9} = \frac{5}{6}$ _____

6. $y - \frac{7}{8} = -\frac{15}{16}$ _____

7. $h + 2\frac{1}{2} = -1\frac{1}{4}$ _____

8. $n - 3\frac{2}{5} = -1\frac{7}{10}$ _____

9. $f + 4\frac{3}{8} = 2\frac{1}{3}$ _____

10. $b - 1\frac{2}{5} = 1\frac{4}{7}$ _____

Practice 5-7 Solving Equations by Adding or Subtracting Fractions

Solve each equation.

1. $m - \left(-\frac{7}{10}\right) = -1\frac{1}{5}$ _____

2. $k - \frac{3}{4} = \frac{2}{5}$ _____

3. $x - \frac{5}{6} = \frac{1}{10}$ _____

4. $t - \left(-3\frac{1}{6}\right) = 7\frac{2}{3}$ _____

5. $x + \frac{5}{8} = \frac{7}{8}$ _____

6. $k + \frac{4}{5} = 1\frac{3}{5}$ _____

7. $4 = \frac{4}{9} + y$ _____

8. $h + \left(-\frac{5}{8}\right) = -\frac{5}{12}$ _____

9. $n + \frac{2}{3} = \frac{1}{9}$ _____

10. $e - \frac{11}{16} = -\frac{7}{8}$ _____

11. $w - 14\frac{1}{12} = -2\frac{3}{4}$ _____

12. $v + \left(-4\frac{5}{6}\right) = 2\frac{1}{3}$ _____

13. $a - 9\frac{1}{6} = -3\frac{19}{24}$ _____

14. $f + \left|-3\frac{11}{12}\right| = 18$ _____

15. $z + \left(-3\frac{2}{5}\right) = -4\frac{1}{10}$ _____

16. $x - \frac{7}{15} = \frac{7}{60}$ _____

17. $h - \left(-6\frac{1}{2}\right) = 14\frac{1}{4}$ _____

18. $p - 5\frac{3}{8} = -\frac{11}{24}$ _____

Solve each equation using mental math.

19. $x + \frac{3}{7} = \frac{5}{7}$ _____

20. $k - \frac{8}{9} = -\frac{1}{9}$ _____

21. $a + \frac{1}{9} = \frac{3}{9}$ _____

22. $g - \frac{4}{5} = -\frac{2}{5}$ _____

Write an equation to solve each problem.

23. Pete's papaya tree grew $3\frac{7}{12}$ ft during the year. If its height at the end of the year was $21\frac{1}{6}$ ft, what was its height at the beginning of the year?

_____

24. Lee is $1\frac{3}{4}$ ft taller than Jay. If Lee is $6\frac{1}{4}$ ft tall, how tall is Jay?

_____

Reteaching 5-8 Solving Equations by Multiplying Fractions

Solve $-4\frac{2}{5}x = 1\frac{1}{10}$.

$$-4\frac{2}{5}x = 1\frac{1}{10}$$

$$-\frac{22}{5}x = \frac{11}{10}$$

Write $-4\frac{2}{5}$ as $-\frac{22}{5}$ and $1\frac{1}{10}$ as $\frac{11}{10}$.

$$-\frac{5}{22} \cdot -\frac{22}{5}x = -\frac{5}{22} \cdot \frac{11}{10}$$

Multiply each side by $-\frac{5}{22}$, the reciprocal of $-\frac{22}{5}$.

$$x = -\frac{\overset{1}{\cancel{5}}}{\underset{2}{\cancel{22}}} \cdot \frac{\overset{1}{\cancel{11}}}{\underset{2}{\cancel{10}}} = -\frac{1}{4}$$

Divide common factors and simplify.

Solve each equation.

1. $8x = 12$ _____

2. $\frac{1}{2}x = \frac{3}{4}$ _____

3. $-\frac{4}{5}y = -\frac{1}{3}$ _____

4. $5h = -\frac{10}{11}$ _____

5. $-\frac{3}{14}j = -1\frac{2}{7}$ _____

6. $\frac{4}{5}p = 2\frac{3}{10}$ _____

7. $1\frac{3}{7}m = \frac{6}{7}$ _____

8. $-\frac{5}{9}n = 2\frac{2}{3}$ _____

9. $4\frac{1}{2}x = 5\frac{5}{8}$ _____

10. $-1\frac{2}{3}k = 4\frac{1}{6}$ _____

Practice 5-8 *Solving Equations by Multiplying Fractions*

Solve each equation.

1. $\frac{3}{4}x = \frac{9}{16}$ _____

2. $-\frac{1}{3}p = \frac{1}{4}$ _____

3. $\frac{-3}{8}k = \frac{1}{2}$ _____

4. $\frac{1}{8}h = \frac{1}{10}$ _____

5. $2\frac{2}{3}e = \frac{1}{18}$ _____

6. $-1\frac{2}{7}m = 6$ _____

7. $-\frac{1}{4}p = \frac{1}{18}$ _____

8. $\frac{11}{-12}w = -1$ _____

9. $-3\frac{4}{7}x = 0$ _____

10. $\frac{2}{3}m = 2\frac{2}{9}$ _____

11. $5c = \frac{2}{3}$ _____

12. $-8k = \frac{4}{5}$ _____

13. $\frac{4}{7}y = 4$ _____

14. $2\frac{1}{4}f = \frac{6}{5}$ _____

15. $\frac{10}{11}n = \frac{2}{11}$ _____

16. $\frac{7}{8}c = \frac{7}{6}$ _____

Solve each equation using mental math.

17. $7d = 42$ _____

18. $\frac{1}{4}y = 5$ _____

19. $-3h = \frac{3}{8}$ _____

20. $\frac{1}{5}k = -\frac{1}{3}$ _____

Write an equation to solve each problem.

21. It takes Nancy $1\frac{2}{3}$ min to read 1 page in her social studies book. It took her $22\frac{1}{2}$ min to complete her reading assignment. How long was the assignment? Let m represent the number of pages she read.

_____

22. It takes Gary three hours to drive to Boston. If the trip is 156 miles, what is Gary's average number of miles per hour? Let x represent the miles per hour.

_____

Name _____ Class _____ Date _____

Reteaching 5-9 Powers of Products and Quotients

Simplify $\left(\frac{x^3}{-y^2}\right)^5$.

$$\left(\frac{x^3}{-y^2}\right)^5 = \frac{(x^3)^5}{(-y^2)^5}$$ Raise both the numerator and the denominator to the power of 5.

$$= \frac{x^{15}}{(-1)^5(y^2)^5}$$ Multiply exponents in the numerator. Raise each factor to the power of 5 in the denominator.

$$= -\frac{x^{15}}{y^{10}}$$ Multiply exponents and simplify.

Simplify each expression.

1. $(2 \cdot 5)^4$ _____

2. $(-3 \cdot 2)^3$ _____

3. $(4x)^2$ _____

4. $(a^2b)^5$ _____

5. $(3ab^3)^2$ _____

6. $-(5m^2n^3)^3$ _____

7. $\left(\frac{2}{9}\right)^2$ _____

8. $\left(-\frac{7}{8}\right)^2$ _____

9. $\left(-\frac{3}{10}\right)^3$ _____

10. $\left(\frac{4}{x^4}\right)^2$ _____

11. $\left(\frac{3x}{5}\right)^3$ _____

12. $\left(-\frac{a^2}{b^5}\right)^4$ _____

13. $\left(\frac{xy^2}{2z^3}\right)^5$ _____

14. $\left(\frac{-1}{2n^3}\right)^4$ _____

15. $\left(\frac{-2r^3s}{3t^2}\right)^2$ _____

16. $\left(\frac{-3}{a^2bc^2}\right)^3$ _____

17. $(p^4q^3r^2)^3$ _____

18. $\left(\frac{x^2yz^3}{-2}\right)^4$ _____

19. $\left(\frac{5}{j^3k}\right)^2$ _____

20. $\left(\frac{ac^4}{4b}\right)^3$ _____

Practice 5-9 *Powers of Products and Quotients*

Simplify each expression.

1. $\left(\frac{5}{6}\right)^2$ _____

2. $\left(-\frac{4}{9}\right)^2$ _____

3. $\left(\frac{x^2}{5}\right)^3$ _____

4. $(2x)^3$ _____

5. $(-3y^2)^2$ _____

6. $(5ab^2)^3$ _____

7. $(12mn)^2$ _____

8. $(-10xy^3)^3$ _____

9. $(9qrs^4)^3$ _____

10. $\left(\frac{2x}{9y}\right)^2$ _____

11. $-(a^2b^2)^3$ _____

12. $(2a^3b^2)^4$ _____

13. $\left(\frac{2x}{y}\right)^2$ _____

14. $\left(-\frac{3x}{8y}\right)^2$ _____

15. $\left(\frac{3y^2}{x}\right)^3$ _____

16. $\left(\frac{2x^2y}{xy^3}\right)^5$ _____

Evaluate for $a = 2$, $b = -1$, and $c = \frac{1}{3}$.

17. $(a^2)^3$ _____

18. $2b^3$ _____

19. $(-9c^2)^3$ _____

20. $(a^2b)^2$ _____

21. $(ac)^2$ _____

22. $(b^3)^7$ _____

Complete each equation.

23. $(3b^{\underline{}})^2 = 9b^{10}$

24. $(m^2n)^{\underline{}} = m^8n^4$

25. $(xy^{\underline{}})^2 = x^2y^6$

26. $\left(\frac{3s^2t}{r}\right)^{\underline{}} = \frac{9s^4t^2}{r^2}$

27. Write an expression for the area of a square with a side of length $4a^2$. Simplify your expression.

   _____

28. Write an expression for the volume of a cube with a side of length $3z^5$. Simplify your expression.

   _____

Reteaching 6-1 *Ratios and Unit Rates*

One store has 6-packs of juice for $.90. Another store has 8-packs of the same size juice cartons for $1.12. Which is the better buy?

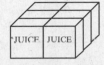 

6-pack
$0.90

8-pack
$1.12

Find the unit rates.

6-pack: $\frac{\text{price} \rightarrow}{\text{number} \rightarrow} \frac{\$.90}{6} = \$.15/\text{carton}$

8-pack: $\frac{\text{price} \rightarrow}{\text{number} \rightarrow} \frac{\$1.12}{8} = \$.14/\text{carton}$

The 8-pack has the lowest unit price.

Find each unit rate.

1. $91 in 14 h

_____

2. 372 mi in 6 h

_____

3. $13.14 for 12 gal

_____

4. 570 gal in 60 min

_____

5. 54¢ for 4 oz

_____

6. 592 words in 8 min

_____

7. A 12 fl oz bottle of shampoo costs $1.08 at Discount Mart. A 20 fl oz bottle of the same shampoo costs $2.20 at Super Store. Find each unit rate and determine which is the better buy.

12 fl oz bottle: _____

20 fl oz bottle: _____

Better buy: _____

8. A school bus travels 53.3 mi on 6.5 gal of gas on its way to a museum for a field trip. On the return trip it takes the freeway and travels 53.2 mi on 5.6 gal of gas. Find the gas mileages of each trip and determine which is greater.

To the museum: _____

Returning from the museum: _____

Better mileage: _____

Practice 6-1 Ratios and Unit Rates

Find each unit rate.

1. 78 mi on 3 gal _____

2. $52.50 in 7 h _____

3. 416 mi in 8 h _____

4. 9 bull's eyes in 117 throws _____

Write each ratio as a fraction in simplest form.

	Boys	Girls
7th Grade	26	34
8th Grade	30	22

5. 7th-grade boys to 8th-grade boys _____

6. 7th-grade girls to 7th-grade boys _____

7. 7th graders to 8th graders _____

8. boys to girls _____

9. girls to all students _____

Write three different ratios for each model.

10.

11. ● ● ●
○ ○

12.

_____ _____ _____

Write each ratio as a fraction in simplest form.

13. 7 : 12 _____   **14.** 3 is to 6 _____

15. 10 : 45 _____   **16.** 32 out of 40 _____

17. 36 is to 60 _____   **18.** 13 out of 14 _____

19. 9 out of 21 _____   **20.** 45 : 63 _____

21. 24 is to 18 _____   **22.** 15 out of 60 _____

Reteaching 6-2 Proportions

Solve $\frac{x}{6} = \frac{10}{4}$

Method 1: Multiplication Property of Equality		Method 2: cross products	
$\frac{x}{6} = \frac{10}{4}$		$\frac{x}{6} \bowtie \frac{10}{4}$	
$\frac{x}{6} \cdot 6 = \frac{10}{4} \cdot 6$	Multiply each side by 6.	$4x = 60$	Find the cross products.
$x = \frac{60}{4}$	Simplify.	$\frac{4x}{4} = \frac{60}{4}$	Divide each side by 4.
$x = 15$		$x = 15$	Simplify.

Solve each proportion. When necessary, round to the nearest hundredth.

1. $\frac{6}{p} = \frac{18}{42}$

_____

2. $\frac{12}{21} = \frac{x}{14}$

_____

3. $\frac{y}{9} = \frac{26}{6}$

_____

4. $\frac{x}{9} = \frac{7}{12}$

_____

5. $\frac{63}{t} = \frac{14}{16}$

_____

6. $\frac{28}{15} = \frac{y}{25}$

_____

7. $\frac{7}{20} = \frac{e}{70}$

_____

8. $\frac{8}{3} = \frac{40}{k}$

_____

9. $\frac{m}{54} = \frac{5}{12}$

_____

10. $\frac{8}{w} = \frac{5}{24}$

_____

11. $\frac{63}{18} = \frac{14}{z}$

_____

12. $\frac{a}{70} = \frac{2}{5}$

_____

13. $\frac{5}{13} = \frac{20}{r}$

_____

14. $\frac{6}{t} = \frac{7}{56}$

_____

15. $\frac{c}{21} = \frac{6}{20}$

_____

16. $\frac{10}{e} = \frac{15}{27}$

_____

Practice 6-2 Proportions

Write a proportion for each phrase. Then solve. When necessary, round to the nearest hundredth.

1. 420 ft^2 painted in 36 min; f ft^2 painted in 30 min

   _____

2. 75 points scored in 6 games; p points scored in 4 games

   _____

3. 6 apples for $1.00; 15 apples for d dollars

   _____

Tell whether each pair of ratios forms a proportion.

4. $\frac{3}{4}$ and $\frac{9}{12}$ _____

5. $\frac{25}{40}$ and $\frac{5}{8}$ _____

6. $\frac{8}{12}$ and $\frac{14}{21}$ _____

7. $\frac{13}{15}$ and $\frac{4}{5}$ _____

8. $\frac{4}{5}$ and $\frac{5}{6}$ _____

9. $\frac{49}{21}$ and $\frac{28}{12}$ _____

Solve each proportion. Where necessary, round to the nearest tenth.

10. $\frac{3}{5} = \frac{15}{x}$ _____

11. $\frac{15}{30} = \frac{n}{34}$ _____

12. $\frac{h}{36} = \frac{21}{27}$ _____

13. $\frac{11}{6} = \frac{f}{60}$ _____

14. $\frac{26}{15} = \frac{130}{m}$ _____

15. $\frac{36}{j} = \frac{7}{20}$ _____

16. $\frac{r}{23} = \frac{17}{34}$ _____

17. $\frac{77}{93} = \frac{x}{24}$ _____

18. At Discount Copy, 12 copies cost $0.66. Melissa needs 56 copies. How much should they cost?

    _____

19. You estimate that you can do 12 math problems in 45 min. How long should it take you to do 20 math problems?

    _____

Reteaching 6-3 *Similar Figures and Scale Drawings*

Similar triangles have the same shape but not necessarily the same size. In the figures, $\triangle ABC$ is similar to $\triangle DEF$.

The symbol $\sim$ means "is similar to." $\triangle ABC \sim \triangle DEF$.

The lengths of the sides of similar triangles are always proportional to each other.

Find *EF*.

Substitute into $\frac{AC}{DF} = \frac{BC}{EF}$.

$\frac{8}{4} = \frac{10}{x}$ Write a proportion.

$8x = 40$ Find the cross products.

$\frac{8x}{8} = \frac{40}{8}$ Divide each side by 8.

$x = 5$ Simplify.

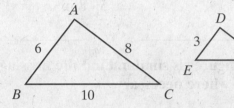

Use the properties of similar triangles to calculate the side lengths in each problem.

1. $\triangle MNP \sim \triangle STW$.

   a. Complete: $\frac{MN}{ST} = \frac{MP}{\rule{1cm}{0.15mm}}$; $\frac{MN}{ST} = \frac{\rule{1cm}{0.15mm}}{TW}$

   b. Substitute the correct lengths in the above proportions and solve.

   $\frac{20}{15} = \frac{36}{SW}$; $\rule{1.5cm}{0.15mm} = \rule{1.5cm}{0.15mm}$

   $SW = $ _____ $NP = $ _____

2. $\triangle DKL \sim \triangle REV$.

   $DK = $ _____

   $RV = $ _____

   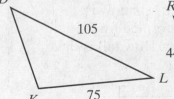

3. $\triangle ANF \sim \triangle KGS$.

   $AN = $ _____

   $GS = $ _____

   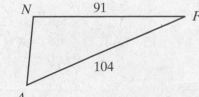
   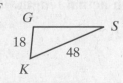
   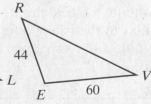

Practice 6-3 Similar Figures and Scale Drawings

The scale of a map is $\frac{1}{2}$ in. : 8 mi. Find the actual distance for each map distance.

1. 2 in.

2. 5 in.

3. $3\frac{1}{2}$ in.

_____

_____

_____

4. 10 in.

5. 8 in.

6. $7\frac{1}{4}$ in.

_____

_____

_____

Each pair of figures is similar. Find the missing length. Round to the nearest tenth where necessary.

7.

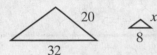

$x =$ _____

8.

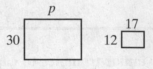

$p =$ _____

9.

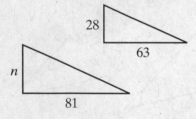

$n =$ _____

10.

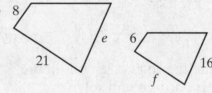

$e \approx$ _____ $f \approx$ _____

11. A meter stick casts a shadow 1.4 m long at the same time a flagpole casts a shadow 7.7 m long. The triangle formed by the meterstick and its shadow is similar to the triangle formed by the flagpole and its shadow. How tall is the flagpole?

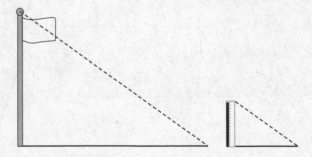

_____

A scale drawing has a scale of $\frac{1}{4}$ in. : 6 ft. Find the length on the drawing for each actual length.

12. 18 ft

13. 66 ft

14. 204 ft

_____

_____

_____

Reteaching 6-4 Probability

Suppose you select a letter at random from the words MIDDLE SCHOOL. Find $P(L)$ and $P(\text{not } L)$.

First determine the number of possible outcomes. There are 12 letters in the two words, so there are 12 possible outcomes when you select a letter at random. Next determine the number of favorable outcomes for $P(L)$. There are two L's.

Thus, $P(L) = \frac{\text{number of favorable outcomes}}{\text{number of possible outcomes}} = \frac{2}{12} = \frac{1}{6}$

You can find $P(\text{not } L)$ several ways. Since there are 12 possible outcomes and 2 are L, $12 - 2 = 10$ are not L.

Thus, $P(\text{not } L) = \frac{\text{number of favorable outcomes}}{\text{number of possible outcomes}} = \frac{10}{12} = \frac{5}{6}$

Also $P(\text{not } L) = 1 - P(L)$

$\qquad\qquad = 1 - \frac{1}{6} = \frac{5}{6}$

A drawer contains 6 red socks, 4 blue socks, and 14 white socks. A sock is pulled from the drawer at random. Find the probability for each case.

1. $P(\text{red})$ _____

2. $P(\text{blue})$ _____

3. $P(\text{red or white})$ _____

4. $P(\text{red, white, or blue})$ _____

5. $P(\text{not red})$ _____

6. $P(\text{green})$ _____

Suppose you spin a spinner that is equally likely to land on any one of the numbers from 1 to 20. Find the probability for each event.

7. $P(17)$

8. $P(\text{an odd number})$

9. $P(\text{a number divisible by 5})$

10. $P(26)$

11. $P(\text{a number with a 1 in it})$

12. $P(\text{a prime number})$

13. $P(\text{a number less than 6})$

14. $P(\text{a number})$

15. $P(\text{a number that is not less than 17})$

16. $P(\text{a number divisible by 3 or 4})$

Practice 6-4 Probability

Find each probability for choosing a letter at random from the word PROBABILITY.

1. P(B) _____

2. P(P) _____

3. P(A or I) _____

4. P(not P) _____

A child is chosen at random from the Erb and Smith families. Find the odds in favor of each of the following being chosen.

5. a girl

_____

6. an Erb

_____

7. an Erb girl

_____

8. a Smith girl

_____

	Erb family	Smith family
Girls	2	5
Boys	4	3

9. not a Smith boy

_____

10. a Smith

_____

A box contains 7 red, 14 yellow, 21 green, 42 blue, and 84 purple marbles. A marble is drawn at random from the box. Find each probability.

11. P(red)

_____

12. P(yellow)

_____

13. P(green or blue)

_____

14. P(purple, yellow, or red)

_____

15. P(not green)

_____

16. P(not purple, yellow, or red)

_____

Find the odds in favor of each selection when a marble is chosen at random from the box described above.

17. blue _____

18. purple _____

19. not red _____

20. not green or blue _____

21. yellow _____

22. not purple or yellow _____

Reteaching 6-5 Fractions, Decimals, and Percents

Write $\frac{7}{8}$ as a percent and 64% as a fraction in lowest terms.

Divide $7 \div 8$.

$$\begin{array}{r} 0.875 \\ 8\overline{)7.000} \\ 6\ 4 \\ \hline 60 \\ 56 \\ \hline 40 \\ 40 \\ \hline \end{array}$$

$\frac{7}{8} = 0.875$

$0.875 = 87.5\%$

Thus $\frac{7}{8} = 87.5\%$.

64% means 64 parts per 100.

$64\% = \frac{64}{100}$

$= \frac{2^4}{2^2 \cdot 5^2}$

$= \frac{16}{25}$

Thus $64\% = \frac{16}{25}$.

Write each fraction as a percent.

1. $\frac{7}{10}$ _____

2. $\frac{3}{5}$ _____

3. $\frac{11}{20}$ _____

4. $\frac{17}{25}$ _____

5. $\frac{1}{5}$ _____

6. $\frac{39}{100}$ _____

7. $\frac{1}{20}$ _____

8. $\frac{13}{50}$ _____

9. $\frac{5}{8}$ _____

10. $\frac{3}{16}$ _____

Write each percent as a fraction in simplest terms.

11. 15% _____

12. 12.5% _____

13. 76% _____

14. 14% _____

15. 60% _____

16. 97% _____

17. 25% _____

18. 30% _____

19. 82% _____

20. 68.75% _____

Practice 6-5 Fractions, Decimals, and Percents

Write each decimal or fraction as a percent. Round to the nearest tenth of a percent where necessary.

1. 0.16 _____

2. 0.72 _____

3. $\frac{24}{25}$ _____

4. $\frac{31}{40}$ _____

5. $\frac{111}{200}$ _____

6. $\frac{403}{1,000}$ _____

7. 3.04 _____

8. 5.009 _____

9. 0.0004 _____

10. $\frac{40}{13}$ _____

11. $\frac{4}{7}$ _____

12. $\frac{57}{99}$ _____

Write each percent as a decimal.

13. 8% _____

14. 12.4% _____

15. 145% _____

16. 0.07% _____

17. $7\frac{1}{2}$% _____

18. $15\frac{1}{4}$% _____

Write each percent as a fraction or mixed number in simplest form.

19. 60% _____

20. 5% _____

21. 35% _____

22. 32% _____

23. 140% _____

24. 0.8% _____

Use >, <, or = to complete each statement.

25. 0.7 ☐ 7%

26. 80% ☐ $\frac{4}{5}$

27. $\frac{1}{3}$ ☐ 33%

28. In the United States in 1990, about one person in twenty was 75 years old or older. Write this fraction as a percent.

_____

Name _____ Class _____ Date _____

Reteaching 6-6 *Proportions and Percents*

What percent of 98 is 24.5?

You can solve percent problems by writing and solving a proportion.

Any percent problem of the form x% of a is b can be written as:

$\frac{x}{100} = \frac{b}{a}$

so $\frac{x}{100} = \frac{24.5}{98}$ Write a proportion.

      $98x = 2,450$ Write cross products.

      $\frac{98x}{98} = \frac{2,450}{98}$ Divide each side by 98.

      $x = 25$ Simplify.

24.5 is 25% of 98.

Write a proportion. Then solve. Where necessary, round to the nearest tenth or tenth of a percent.

1. What percent of 75 is 60?

_____

2. What percent of 68 is 51?

_____

3. What percent is 17 of 25?

_____

4. What percent of 51 is 65?

_____

5. What percent of 144 is 126?

_____

6. What percent of 95 is 25?

_____

7. Find 24% of 120.

_____

8. Find 75% of 76.

_____

9. Find 260% of 30.

_____

10. Find $27\frac{1}{2}$% of 96.

_____

11. Find 38% of 32.

_____

12. Find 17% of 85.

_____

13. 40% of x is 28. What is x?

_____

14. 9% of k is 27. What is k?

_____

15. 75% of p is 12. What is p?

_____

16. 0.9% of h is 276. What is h?

_____

17. 13% of r is 209. What is r?

_____

18. .68% of j is 44. What is j?

_____

Practice 6-6 Proportions and Percents

Write a proportion. Then solve. Where necessary, round to the nearest tenth or tenth of a percent.

1. $62\frac{1}{2}\%$ of t is 35. What is t? _____

2. 38% of n is 33.44. What is n? _____

3. 120% of y is 42. What is y? _____

4. 300% of m is 600. What is m? _____

5. 1.5% of h is 12. What is h? _____

6. What percent of 40 is 12? _____

7. What percent of 48 is 18? _____

8. What percent is 54 of 60? _____

9. What percent is 39 of 50? _____

10. Find 80% of 25. _____

11. Find 150% of 74. _____

12. Find 44% of 375. _____

13. Find 65% of 180. _____

14. The Eagles won 70% of the 40 games that they played. How many games did they win?

_____

15. Thirty-five of 40 students surveyed said that they favored recycling. What percent of those surveyed favored recycling?

_____

16. Candidate Carson received 2,310 votes, 55% of the total. How many total votes were cast?

_____

Reteaching 6-7 Percents and Equations

You can solve percent problems by writing and solving an equation.

8 is 16% of what?

$8 = 0.16 \cdot n$ Write an equation. Write the percent as a decimal.

$\frac{8}{0.16} = \frac{0.16n}{0.16}$ Divide each side by 0.16.

$50 = n$ Simplify

8 is 16% of 50.

Write and solve an equation. Where necessary, round to the nearest tenth or tenth of a percent.

1. What percent is 84 of 60?

   _____

2. What percent of 40 is 26?

   _____

3. What percent is 22 of 33?

   _____

4. What percent of 32 is 28?

   _____

5. What percent is 18 of 48?

   _____

6. What percent of 81 is 18?

   _____

7. Find 37.5% of 104.

   _____

8. Find 0.4% of 25.

   _____

9. Find 68% of 150.

   _____

10. Find 180% of 65.

   _____

11. Find 12.5% of 56.

   _____

12. Find 86% of 55.

   _____

13. 95% of h is 60. What is h?

   _____

14. 24% of m is 17. What is m?

   _____

15. 30% of n is 42. What is n?

   _____

16. 28% of b is 49. What is b?

   _____

17. 25% of y is 96. What is y?

   _____

18. 72% of k is 234. What is k?

   _____

Practice 6-7 *Percents and Equations*

Write and solve an equation. Where necessary, round to the nearest tenth or tenth of a percent.

1. What percent of 25 is 17? _____

2. What percent is 10 of 8? _____

3. What percent is 63 of 84? _____

4. What percent is 3 of 600? _____

5. Find 45% of 60. _____

6. Find 325% of 52. _____

7. Find $66\frac{2}{3}$% of 87. _____

8. Find 1% of 3,620. _____

9. $62\frac{1}{2}$% of x is 5. What is x? _____

10. 300% of k is 42. What is k? _____

11. $33\frac{1}{3}$% of p is 19. What is p? _____

12. 70% of c is 49. What is c? _____

13. 15% of n is 1,050. What is n? _____

14. 38% of y is 494. What is y? _____

15. A camera regularly priced at $295 was placed on sale at $236. What percent of the regular price was the sale price?

    _____

16. Nine hundred thirty-six students, 65% of the entire student body, attended the football game. Find the size of the student body.

    _____

Reteaching 6-8 Percent of Change

Find the percent of decrease from 85 to 60.

Find the amount of decrease.

$85 - 60 = 25$

percent of decrease $= \dfrac{\text{amount of decrease}}{\text{original amount}}$

$ = \dfrac{25}{85}$

$ \approx 0.294 = 29.4\%$

The percent of decrease is about 29.4%

Find each percent of increase. Where necessary, round to the nearest tenth of a percent.

1. 40 is increased to 45.

2. 33 is increased to 55.

3. 15 is increased to 34.

4. 11 is increased to 88.

5. 72 is increased to 117.

6. 28 is increased to 49.

7. 35 is increased to 49.

8. 48 is increased to 132.

Find each percent of decrease. Where necessary, round to the nearest tenth of a percent.

9. 60 is decreased to 15.

10. 56 is decreased to 35.

11. 140 is decreased to 77.

12. 96 is decreased to 64.

13. 99 is decreased to 69.

14. 50 is decreased to 44.

15. 83 is decreased to 0.

16. 475 is decreased to 152.

Practice 6-8 Percent of Change

Find each percent of change. Round to the nearest tenth of a percent. Tell whether the change is an increase or a decrease.

1. 24 to 21 _____   **2.** 64 to 80 _____

3. 100 to 113 _____   **4.** 50 to 41 _____

5. 63 to 105 _____   **6.** 42 to 168 _____

7. 80 to 24 _____   **8.** 200 to 158 _____

9. 56 to 71 _____   **10.** 127 to 84 _____

11. 20 to 24 _____   **12.** 44 to 22 _____

13. 16 to 12 _____   **14.** 10 to 100 _____

15. 20 to 40 _____   **16.** 10 to 50 _____

17. 12 to 16 _____   **18.** 80 to 100 _____

19. 69 to 117 _____   **20.** 19 to 9 _____

21. 95 to 145 _____   **22.** 88 to 26 _____

23. Mark weighed 110 pounds last year. He weighs 119 pounds this year. What is the percent of increase in his weight, to the nearest tenth of a percent?

_____

24. Susan had $140 in her savings account last month. She added $20 this month and earned $.50 interest. What is the percent of increase in the amount in her savings account to the nearest tenth of a percent?

_____

25. The population density of California was 151.4 people per square mile in 1980. By 1990 it had increased to 190.8 people per square mile. Find the percent increase to the nearest percent.

_____

Reteaching 6-9 *Markup and Discount*

A store pays $8 for a basketball. The markup is 60%. Later, they discount the basketball 25%. Find the original selling price and the sale price of the basketball.

Method 1

The markup is 60% of the cost.
Find 60% of $8.
$0.6(8) = \$4.80$
Store's cost + markup = selling price
$8 + 4.80 = \$12.80$
The original selling price is $12.80.

The discount is 25% of the original selling price.
Find 25% of $12.80
$0.25(12.80) = 3.20$
original price − discount = sale price
$12.80 − 3.20 − 9.60$
The sale price is $9.60

Method 2

The selling price equals 100% of the cost plus 60% (the markup) of the cost, or 160%.
Find 160% of $8.
$1.60(8) = \$12.80$
The original selling price is $12.80.

The sale price is 100% of the original price minus 25% of the original price, or 75%.
Find 75% of $12.80
$0.75(12.80) = \$9.60$
The sale price is $9.60

Complete each table. Where necessary, round to the nearest cent.

	Cost	Markup	Selling Price
1.	$17	50%	
2.	$48	70%	
3.	$110	85%	
4.	$87	65%	
5.	$335	35%	

	Original Selling Price	Discount	Sale Price
6.	$19	25%	
7.	$136	15%	
8.	$849	30%	
9.	$29.99	40%	
10.	$2.59	35%	

Practice 6-9 Markup and Discount

Find each sale price. Round to the nearest cent where necessary.

	Regular Price	Percent of Discount	Sale Price
1.	$46	25%	
2.	$35.45	15%	
3.	$174	40%	
4.	$1.40	30%	
5.	$87	50%	
6.	$675	20%	

Find each selling price. Round to the nearest cent where necessary.

	Cost	Percent Markup	Selling Price
7.	$5.50	75%	
8.	$25	50%	
9.	$170	85%	
10.	$159.99	70%	
11.	$12.65	90%	
12.	$739	20%	

13. A company buys a sweater for $14 and marks it up 90%. It later discounts the sweater 25%.

   a. Find the selling price of the sweater after markup.

   _____

   b. How much was the discount?

   _____

   c. Find the sale price after the discount.

   _____

   d. The company's profit on the sweater can be found by subtracting the final selling price minus the cost. What was the company's profit on the sweater?

   _____

   e. The profit was what percent of the cost?

   _____

Reteaching 6-10 *Make a Table*

A saving account pays 4% interest per year. You deposit $1,000 and then do not deposit or withdraw any money. How much will be in the account at the end of 5 years?

A table can help you solve the problem.

Year	Beginning Balance	Interest	Ending Balance
1	$1,000	$40	$1,040
2	$1,040	$41.60	$1,081.60
3	$1,081.60	$43.26	$1,124.86
4	$1,124.86	$44.99	$1,169.85
5	$1,169.85	$46.79	$1,216.64

The first year, your interest is 4% of $1,000 or $40. At the end of the first year and the beginning of the second year, you have $1,040. The second year, your interest is 4% of $1,040 or $41.60. If you finish the table, you find you have $1,216.64 at the end of 5 years.

A savings account pays 5% interest per year. You deposit $1,800 and then do not deposit or withdraw any money. Complete the table to find out how much will be in the account at the end of 10 years.

	Year	Beginning Balance	Interest	Ending Balance
1.	1	$1,800		
2.	2			
3.	3			
4.	4			
5.	5			
6.	6			
7.	7			
8.	8			
9.	9			
10.	10			

Amount: _____

Practice 6-10 Make a Table

Make a table to solve each problem.

1. A car was worth $12,500 in 1998. Its value depreciates, or decreases, 15% per year. Find its value in 2002.

Year	1998	1999	2000	2001	2002
Car's Value	$12,500				

2. Marcus spent $105 on 6 items at a sale. Videotapes were on sale for $15 each and music CDs were on sale for $20 each. How many of each item did Marcus buy?

Number of Videotapes	1	2	3	4	5
Number of CD's	5	4	3	2	1
Total Cost					

_____

3. Karina likes to mix either apple, orange, or grape juice with either lemon-lime soft drink or sparkling water to make a fizz. How many different fizzes can she make?

_____

4. How many ways can you have 25 cents in change?

_____

5. The deer population of a state park has increased 8% a year for the last 4 years. If there are 308 deer in the park this year, find how large the population was 4 years ago by completing the table.

Year		1	2	3	4
Deer Population					308

6. How many different sandwiches can you make from 3 types of bread, 2 types of cheese, and 2 types of meat? Assume that only one type of each item is used per sandwich.

_____

7. A bus leaves a station at 8:00 A.M. and averages 30 mi/h. Another bus leaves the same station following the same route two hours after the first and averages 50 mi/h. When will the second bus catch up with the first bus?

_____

Reteaching 7-1 Solving Two-Step Equations

Solve $\frac{k}{5} - 9 = -7$.

$\frac{k}{5} - 9 = -7$	
$\frac{k}{5} - 9 + 9 = -7 + 9$	Add 9 to each side.
$\frac{k}{5} = 2$	Simplify.
$\frac{k}{5} \cdot 5 = 2 \cdot 5$	Multiply each side by 5.
$k = 10$	Simplify.

Complete the example.

1. $4n + 13 = 1$

_____   Subtract 13 from each side.

_____   Simplify.

_____   Divide each side by 4.

_____   Simplify.

Solve each equation.

2. $3x - 5 = 10$ $x = $ _____

3. $\frac{n}{2} + 10 = 7$ $n = $ _____

4. $\frac{m}{7} - 9 = -5$ $m = $ _____

5. $5w - 2 = -12$ $w = $ _____

6. $4a + 12 = -8$ $a = $ _____

7. $\frac{b}{3} + 8 = -7$ $b = $ _____

■ *Practice 7-1* Solving Two-Step Equations

Solve each equation.

1. $4x - 17 = 31$ _____

2. $15 = 2m + 3$ _____

3. $\frac{k}{3} + 3 = 8$ _____

4. $7 = 3 + \frac{h}{6}$ _____

5. $9n + 18 = 81$ _____

6. $5 = \frac{y}{3} - 9$ _____

7. $14 = 5k - 31$ _____

8. $\frac{t}{9} - 7 = -5$ _____

9. $\frac{v}{8} - 9 = -13$ _____

10. $25 - 13f = -14$ _____

Solve each equation using mental math.

11. $3p + 5 = 14$ _____

12. $\frac{k}{2} - 5 = 1$ _____

13. $\frac{m}{7} - 3 = 0$ _____

14. $10v - 6 = 24$ _____

15. $8 + \frac{x}{2} = -7$ _____

16. $7 = 6r - 17$ _____

Choose the correct equation. Solve.

17. Tehira has read 110 pages of a 290-page book. She reads 20 pages each day. How many days will it take to finish?

A. $20 + 110p = 290$

B. $20p + 290 = 110$

C. $110 + 20p = 290$

D. $290 = 110 - 20p$

_____

Write an equation to describe the situation. Solve.

18. A waitress earned $73 for 6 hours of work. The total included $46 in tips. What was her hourly wage?

_____

_____

19. You used $6\frac{3}{4}$ c of sugar while baking muffins and nutbread for a class party. You used a total of $1\frac{1}{2}$ c of sugar for the muffins. Your nutbread recipe calls for $1\frac{3}{4}$ c of sugar per loaf. How many loaves of nutbread did you make?

_____

_____

Reteaching 7-2 Solving Multi-Step Equations

Solve $6 - 2(x + 5) = 8$

$6 - 2(x + 5) = 8$	
$6 - 2x - 10 = 8$	Distribute.
$-2x - 4 = 8$	Simplify. Think of $6 - 2x$ as $6 + (-2x)$. Then subtract $6 - 10$.
$-2x - 4 + 4 = 8 + 4$	Add 4 to each side.
$-2x = 12$	Simplify.
$\frac{-2x}{-2} = \frac{12}{-2}$	Divide each side by -2.
$x = -6$	Simplify.

Solve each equation.

1. $3(a - 4) = 9$

_____ Distribute.

_____ Add 12 to each side.

_____ Simplify.

_____ Divide each side by 3.

_____ Simplify.

Solve each equation.

2. $n + 5n = 30$ $n =$ _____

3. $y - 4y = 33$ $y =$ _____

4. $12 = 4(b - 2)$ $b =$ _____

5. $-3(k - 4) = -6$ $k =$ _____

6. $m - 3m + 3 = 11$ $m =$ _____

7. $2(x - 9) + 5 = 1$ $x =$ _____

■ Practice 7-2 Solving Multi-Step Equations

Solve and check each equation.

1. $\frac{p}{3} - 7 = -2$

_____

2. $2(n - 7) + 3 = 9$

_____

3. $0 = 5(k + 9)$

_____

4. $4h + 7h - 16 = 6$

_____

5. $3(2n - 7) = 9$

_____

6. $-27 = 8x - 5x$

_____

7. $4p + 5 - 7p = -1$

_____

8. $7 - y + 5y = 9$

_____

9. $8e + 3(5 - e) = 10$

_____

10. $-37 = 3x + 11 - 7x$

_____

11. $9 - 3(n - 5) = 30$

_____

12. $\frac{1}{6}(y + 42) - 15 = -3$

_____

Write and solve an equation for each situation.

13. Find three consecutive integers whose sum is 51.

_____

_____

14. Find three consecutive integers whose sum is −15.

_____

_____

15. Find four consecutive integers whose sum is 30.

_____

_____

16. Jack's overtime wage is $3 per hour more than his regular hourly wage. He worked for 5 hours at his regular wage and 4 hours at the overtime wage. He earned $66. Find his regular wage.

_____

Reteaching 7-3 Multi-Step Equations With Fractions and Decimals

Solve $0.25x - 0.4 = 1.6$

You can clear the decimals first. Since 0.25 is the decimal with the greatest number of decimal places and $0.25 = \frac{25}{100}$, multiply each side by 100.

$$0.25x - 0.4 = 1.6$$

$100(0.25x - 0.4) = 100(1.6)$	Multiply each side by 100.
$25x - 40 = 160$	Distribute and simplify.
$25x - 40 + 40 = 160 + 40$	Add 40 to each side.
$25x = 200$	Simplify.
$\frac{25x}{25} = \frac{200}{25}$	Divide each side by 25.
$x = 8$	Simplify.

Solve each equation.

1. $0.8x + 2.1 = 5.3$

2. $0.5k - 3.4 = 0.1$

$x =$ _____

$k =$ _____

3. $2.7n + 4.1 = 36.5$

4. $0.96m - 1.8m = -12.6$

$n =$ _____

$m =$ _____

5. $0.7b + 6 - 0.3b = 6.8$

6. $1.4a + 3.5a - 4.3 = 44.7$

$b =$ _____

$a =$ _____

Practice 7-3 Multi-Step Equations With Fractions and Decimals

Solve and check each equation.

1. $0.7n - 1.5 + 7.3n = 14.5$

   _____

2. $18p - 45 = 0$

   _____

3. $16.3k + 19.2 + 7.5k = -64.1$

   _____

4. $h + 3h + 4h = 100$

   _____

5. $40 - 5n = -2$

   _____

6. $14 = \frac{2}{3}(9y - 15)$

   _____

7. $\frac{2}{3}y - 6 = 2$

   _____

8. $1.2m + 7.5m + 2.1 = 63$

   _____

9. $\frac{7}{8}h - \frac{5}{8} = 2$

   _____

10. $93.96 = 4.7p + 8.7p - 2.6p$

    _____

11. $9w - 16.3 = 5.3$

    _____

12. $88.1 - 2.3f = 72.46$

    _____

13. $-15.3 = -7.5k + 55.2$

    _____

14. $26e + 891 = -71$

    _____

15. $2.3(x + 1.4) = -9.66$

    _____

16. $(x - 17.7) + 19.6 = 27.8$

    _____

Write an equation to describe each situation. Solve.

17. Jolene bought three blouses at one price and 2 blouses priced $3 below the others. The total cost was $91.50. Find the prices of the blouses.

    _____

18. A car rented for $29 per day plus $.08 per mile. Julia paid $46.12 for a one-day rental. How far did she drive?

    _____

By what number would you multiply each equation to clear denominators or decimals? Do not solve.

19. $\frac{1}{3}z + \frac{1}{6} = 5\frac{1}{6}$

20. $3.7 + 2.75k = 27.35$

    _____

Reteaching 7-4 Write an Equation

Write an equation. Then solve.

Orlando worked for $6/h one week and $7/h the next week. He worked 5 more hours the second week than the first and earned $347 for the 2 weeks of work. How many hours did he work each week.

Let h be the number of hours Orlando worked the first week.

Then he worked $h + 5$ hours the second week. He earned $6h$ dollars the first week.

Words	Earnings week 1	+	Earnings week 2	=	Total earnings

↓

Equation	$6h$	+	$7(h + 5)$	=	347

Now solve.

$6h + 7(h + 5) = 347$	
$6h + 7h + 35 = 347$	Distribute.
$13h + 35 = 347$	Simplify.
$13h + 35 - 35 = 347 - 35$	Subtract 35 from each side.
$13h = 312$	Simplify.
$\frac{13h}{13} = \frac{312}{13}$	Divide each side by 13.
$h = 24$	

Orlando worked 24 hours the first week. He worked $h + 5 = 24 + 5 = 29$ hours the second week.

Check: $24 \cdot 6 + 29 \cdot 7 = 144 + 203 = 347$.

Write an equation. Then solve.

1. The sum of half of a number and 8 less than the number is 25.

   _____

   _____

2. A triangle has two sides equal in length and a third side 5 in. longer than half the length of each of the other two sides. If the perimeter of the triangle is 50 in., how long is each side?

   _____

   _____

   _____

Practice 7-4 *Write an Equation*

Write an equation. Then solve.

1. Bill purchased 4 pens for $3.32, including $.16 sales tax. Find the cost of 1 pen.

   _____

   _____

2. Arnold had $1.70 in dimes and quarters. He had 3 more dimes than quarters. How many of each coin did he have?

   _____

   _____

3. A baby weighed 3.2 kg at birth. She gained 0.17 kg per week. How old was she when she weighed 5.75 kg?

   _____

   _____

4. In the parking lot at a truck stop there were 6 more cars than 18-wheel trucks. There were 134 wheels in the parking lot. How many cars and trucks were there?

   _____

   _____

5. The product of 6 and 3 more than k is 48.

   _____

6. A bottle and a cap together cost $1.10. The bottle costs $1 more than the cap. How much does each cost?

   _____

   _____

7. The perimeter of a rectangular garden is 40 ft. The width is 2 ft more than one half the length. Find the length and width.

   _____

   _____

Reteaching 7-5 Solving Equations With Variables on Both Sides

Solve $4(n - 5) + 2 = 3n - 4$.

$4(n - 5) + 2 = 3n - 4$	
$4n - 20 + 2 = 3n - 4$	Distribute.
$4n - 18 = 3n - 4$	Simplify.
$4n - 3n - 18 = 3n - 3n - 4$	Subtract $3n$ from each side.
$n - 18 = -4$	Simplify.
$n - 18 + 18 = -4 + 18$	Add 18 to each side.
$n = 14$	Simplify.

Solve each equation.

1. $7x + 9 = 4x$

2. $8m - 5 = 5m + 7$

$x =$ _____

$m =$ _____

3. $k + k + k = k + 18$

4. $3(n - 5) = -2n$

$k =$ _____

$n =$ _____

5. $4(y - 9) = 3(2y - 8)$

6. $6(z - 2) + 3 = 3z - 15$

$y =$ _____

$z =$ _____

7. $x + 7x + 15x = 29x + 18$

8. $8(7 - p) - 8 = -16(p - 2)$

$x =$ _____

$p =$ _____

■ Practice 7-5 Solving Equations With Variables on Both Sides

Solve each equation.

1. $3k + 16 = 5k$

   _____

2. $5e = 3e + 36$

   _____

3. $n + 4n - 22 = 7n$

   _____

4. $2(x - 7) = 3x$

   _____

5. $8h - 10h = 3h + 25$

   _____

6. $7n + 6n - 5 = 4n + 4$

   _____

7. $11(p - 3) = 5(p + 3)$

   _____

8. $9(m + 2) = -6(m + 7)$

   _____

9. $y + 2(y - 5) = 2y + 2$

   _____

10. $-9x + 7 = 3x + 19$

   _____

11. $k + 9 = 6(k - 11)$

   _____

12. $-6(4 - t) = 12t$

   _____

13. $2(x + 7) = 5(x - 7)$

   _____

14. $5m + 9 = 3(m - 5) + 7$

   _____

15. $5x + 7 = 6x$

   _____

16. $k + 12 = 3k$

   _____

17. $8m = 5m + 12$

   _____

18. $3p - 9 = 4p$

   _____

Write an equation for each situation. Solve.

19. The difference when 7 less than a number is subtracted from twice the number is 12. What is the number?

   _____

   _____

20. Four less than three times a number is three more than two times the number. What is the number?

   _____

   _____

Reteaching 7-6 Solving Two-Step Inequalities

Solve and graph $2x + 9 > 5$.

$2x + 9 > 5$

$2x + 9 - 9 > 5 - 9$ Subtract 9 from each side.

$2x > -4$ Simplify.

$\frac{2x}{2} > \frac{-4}{2}$ Divide each side by 2.

$x > -2$ Simplify.

Since $x > -2$, -2 is not a solution. Use an open circle at -2. Then shade everything to the right of -2.

$$\xleftarrow{\quad} \; -5 \; -4 \; -3 \; \overset{\circ}{-2} \; -1 \; 0 \; 1 \; 2 \; 3 \; 4 \; 5 \; \xrightarrow{\quad}$$

Solve each inequality. Graph the solutions on a number line.

1. $8 + 3x \le 2$ _____

2. $\frac{x}{5} - 3 > -4$ _____

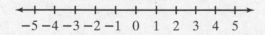

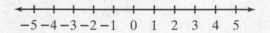

3. $15 - 5k \ge 0$ _____

4. $9 + 2y < 7$ _____

$$\xleftarrow{\quad} \; -5 \; -4 \; -3 \; -2 \; -1 \; 0 \; 1 \; 2 \; 3 \; 4 \; 5 \; \xrightarrow{\quad}$$

$$\xleftarrow{\quad} \; -5 \; -4 \; -3 \; -2 \; -1 \; 0 \; 1 \; 2 \; 3 \; 4 \; 5 \; \xrightarrow{\quad}$$

5. $\frac{x}{2} + 12 > 10$ _____

6. $6t - 5 \ge -23$ _____

$$\xleftarrow{\quad} \; -5 \; -4 \; -3 \; -2 \; -1 \; 0 \; 1 \; 2 \; 3 \; 4 \; 5 \; \xrightarrow{\quad}$$

$$\xleftarrow{\quad} \; -5 \; -4 \; -3 \; -2 \; -1 \; 0 \; 1 \; 2 \; 3 \; 4 \; 5 \; \xrightarrow{\quad}$$

Practice 7-6 Solving Two-Step Inequalities

Solve each inequality. Graph the solutions on a number line.

1. $5x + 2 \leq 17$ _____

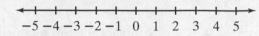
−5 −4 −3 −2 −1 0 1 2 3 4 5

2. $7x + 2x \geq 21 - 3$ _____

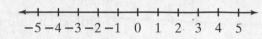
−5 −4 −3 −2 −1 0 1 2 3 4 5

3. $9 - x > 10$ _____
−5 −4 −3 −2 −1 0 1 2 3 4 5

4. $19 + 8 \leq 6 + 7x$ _____
−5 −4 −3 −2 −1 0 1 2 3 4 5

5. $-6x < 12$ _____
−5 −4 −3 −2 −1 0 1 2 3 4 5

6. $\frac{x}{-4} > 0$ _____
−5 −4 −3 −2 −1 0 1 2 3 4 5

Solve each inequality.

7. $2x - 5 > 1$ _____

8. $9x - 7 \leq 38$ _____

9. $3 < \frac{1}{2}x + 1$ _____

10. $-12 < -12x$ _____

11. $-8x + 18 > -22$ _____

12. $50 < 8 - 6x$ _____

13. $\frac{1}{5}x + 6 > -3$ _____

14. $30 \geq -6(5 - x)$ _____

Write an inequality for each situation. Then solve the inequality.

15. Nine more than half the number n is no more than −8. Find n.

_____

_____

16. Judith drove h hours at a rate of 55 mi/h. She did not reach her goal of driving 385 miles for the day. How long did she drive?

_____

_____

Reteaching 7-7 Transforming Formulas

Solve the surface area formula $s = 2\pi r^2 + 2\pi rh$ for h.

$$s = 2\pi r^2 + 2\pi rh$$

$s - 2\pi r^2 = 2\pi r^2 - 2\pi r^2 + 2\pi rh$ Subtract $2\pi r^2$ from each side.

$s - 2\pi r^2 = 2\pi rh$ Simplify.

$\frac{s - 2\pi r^2}{2\pi r} = \frac{2\pi rh}{2\pi r}$ Divide each side by $2\pi r$.

$\frac{s - 2\pi r^2}{2\pi r} = h$ Simplify.

Solve for the indicated variable.

1. $y = mx + b$, for x

2. $y = mx + b$, for m

3. $p = 6s$, for s

4. $A = \frac{1}{2}h(B + b)$, for h

5. $I = Prt$, for P

6. $y = \frac{2}{3}x - 5$, for x

7. $t = 0.05p$, for p

8. $V = lwh$, for w

9. $k = \frac{1}{2}mv^2$, for m

10. $W = p(V - L)$, for V

11. $F = \frac{Gm_1m_2}{r^2}$, for G

12. $W = p(V - L)$, for L

13. $V = \frac{h}{e}v - \frac{E}{e}$, for e

14. $mv = (m + M)u$, for m

Practice 7-7 Transforming Formulas

Use this information to answer Exercises 1–4: Shopping City has a 6% sales tax.

1. Solve the formula $c = 1.06p$ for p, where c is the cost of an item at Shopping City, including tax, and p is the selling price.

   _____

2. Clara spent \$37.10 on a pair of pants at Shopping City. What was the selling price of the pants?

   _____

3. Manuel spent \$10.59 on a basketball at Shopping City. What was the selling price of the ball?

   _____

4. Clara and Manuel's parents spent \$165.84 on groceries at Shopping City. How much of that amount was sales tax?

   _____

Transform the formulas.

5. The area of a triangle A can be found with the formula $A = \frac{1}{2}bh$ where b is the length of the base of the triangle and h is the height of the triangle. Solve the formula for h.

   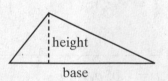

   _____

6. Solve the formula $A = \frac{1}{2}bh$ for b.

   _____

Find the missing part of each triangle.

7. $A = 27 \text{ cm}^2$

   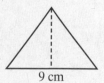

   9 cm

   $h =$ _____

8. $A = 18 \text{ ft}^2$

   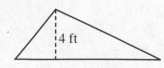

   4 ft

   $b =$ _____

Solve for the variable indicated.

9. $V = \frac{1}{3}lwh$, for w

   _____

10. $\frac{1}{a} + \frac{1}{b} = \frac{1}{c}$, for c

   _____

Reteaching 7-8 Simple and Compound Interest

Find the balance in an account when $500 is deposited at 4% interest compounded semi-annually for 2 years.

The table shows the interest and balance for each half year.

Principal at Beginning of Period	Interest	Balance
$\frac{1}{2}$ year: $500		
1 year:		
$1\frac{1}{2}$ year:		
2 year:		

The balance after 2 years is $541.21.

You can also find the balance with the formula $B = p(1 + r)^n$, where B is the ending balance. The principal p is 500. The rate is for a half year; 4% annual interest equals 2% per half year. Thus r is 0.02. The number of compounding periods n is 4, because there are 4 half years in 2 years.

$B = p(1 + r)^n$
$B = 500(1 + 0.02)^4$ Substitute.
$B = \$541.22$ Use a calculator. Round to the nearest cent.

With the formula, the ending balance is $541.22. The difference is due to rounding error.

Find the ending balance when $1,500 is deposited at 6% interest compounded semi-annually for 2 years.

1. Use a table.

Principal at Beginning of Period	Interest	Balance
$\frac{1}{2}$ year: $1,500		
1 year:		
$1\frac{1}{2}$ year:		
2 year:		

2. Use the formula:
$B = p(1 + r)^n =$ _____ $=$ _____

Practice 7-8 Simple and Compound Interest

Find each balance.

	Principal	Interest rate	Compounded	Time (years)	Balance
1.	$400	7%	annually	3	
2.	$8,000	5%	annually	9	
3.	$1,200	4%	semi-annually	2	
4.	$50,000	6%	semi-annually	6	

Find the simple interest.

5. $900 deposited at an interest rate of 3% for 5 years

_____

6. $1,348 deposited at an interest rate of 2.5% for 18 months

_____

Complete each table. Compound the interest annually.

7. $5,000 at 6% for 4 years.

Principal at beginning of year	Interest	Balance
Year 1: $5,000		
Year 2:		
Year 3:		
Year 4:		

8. $7,200 at 3% for 4 years

Principal at beginning of year	Interest	Balance
Year 1: $7,200		
Year 2:		
Year 3:		
Year 4:		

Reteaching 8-1 Relations and Functions

Graph the relation. Is the relation a function? Explain.

x	y
3	4
−1	2
4	−3
−4	−2

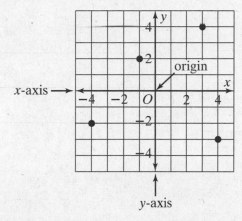

First, plot the point $(3, 4)$. Start at the origin, where the x-axis and the y-axis cross. Go right 3 units and up 4 units.

To plot $(−1, 2)$, from the origin go left one unit and up 2 units.

To plot $(4, −3)$, from the origin, go right 4 units and down 3 units.

To plot $(−4, −2)$, from the origin, go left 4 units and down 2 units.

Next, use the vertical line test. Hold a pencil vertically to the left of the graph. Slowly move it to the right. If you can find a vertical line that passes through two graphed points, then the relation is not a function. If you cannot find such a line, the relation *is* a function. This relation is a function because the vertical pencil does not pass through two points anywhere on the graph.

Graph the relation. Is the relation a function? Explain.

x	y
−4	1
1	3
4	0
1	−2

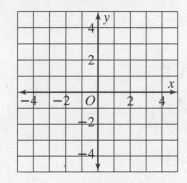

_____

_____

Practice 8-1 Relations and Functions

Graph each relation. Is the relation a function? Explain.

1.

x	y
−1	4
2	3
4	−1
−1	−2

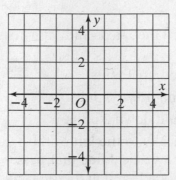

_____

_____

_____

2.

x	y
2	−4
−4	0
−2	3
3	−1

_____

_____

_____

For each relation, list the members of the domain. List the members of the range. Is the relation a function? Explain.

3. {(7, −2), (8, −2), (−5, 7), (−9, 1)}

   Domain: _____   Range: _____

   Function? _____

4. {(−8, 0), (10, 6), (10, −2), (−5, 7)}

   Domain: _____   Range: _____

   Function? _____

5. {(9.2, 4.7), (−3.6, 4.8), (5.2, 4.7)}

   Domain: _____   Range: _____

   Function? _____

6. Is the time is takes you to run a 100-meter race a function of the speed you run? Explain.

   _____

Reteaching 8-2 Equations With Two Variables

Graph $y = \frac{1}{4}x - 2$.

Make a table of ordered pairs. Then graph the ordered pairs and draw a line through the points. Choose values that make computations easy.

x	Substitute and Simplify $y = \frac{1}{4}x - 2$	(x, y)
0	$y = \frac{1}{4}(0) - 2 = 0 - 2 = -2$	$(0, -2)$
4	$y = \frac{1}{4}(4) - 2 = 1 - 2 = -1$	$(4, -1)$
-4	$y = \frac{1}{4}(-4) - 2 = -1 - 2 = -3$	$(-4, -3)$

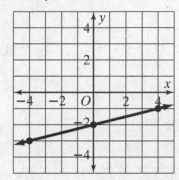

Graph each equation.

1. $y = \frac{3}{2}x - 1$

x	$y = \frac{3}{2}x - 1$	(x, y)
0		
-2		
4		

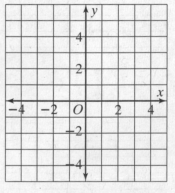

2. $y = x - 3$

x	$y = x - 3$	(x, y)
0		
4		
-1		

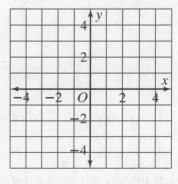

Practice 8-2 Equations With Two Variables

Write each equation as a function in "$y = \ldots$" form.

1. $3y = 15x - 12$ **2.** $5x + 10 = 10y$ **3.** $3y - 21 = 12x$

   $y =$ _____ $y =$ _____ $y =$ _____

4. $5y + 3 = 2y - 3x + 5$ **5.** $-2(x + 3y) = 18$ **6.** $5(x + y) = 20 + 3x$

   $y =$ _____ $y =$ _____ $y =$ _____

Graph each equation.

7. $y = -0.5x + 4$

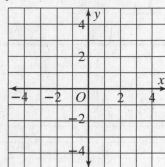

8. $y = 4$

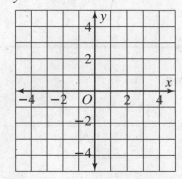

9. $2x - 3y = 6$

   $y =$ _____

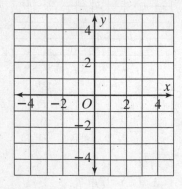

10. $-10x = 5y$

   $y =$ _____

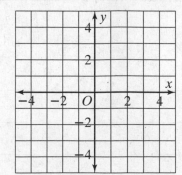

Is each ordered pair a solution of $3x - 2y = 12$? Write *yes* or *no*.

11. $(0, 4)$ _____   **12.** $(6, 3)$ _____   **13.** $(4, 0)$ _____

Is each ordered pair a solution of $-2x + 5y = 10$? Write *yes* or *no*.

14. $(-3, 2)$ _____   **15.** $(-10, -2)$ _____   **16.** $(5, 4)$ _____

Reteaching 8-3 Slope and y-intercept

Find the slope of the line.

Find two points on the line whose coordinates are easy to read, like $(0, -2)$ and $(4, 1)$.

slope $= \frac{rise}{run} = \frac{3}{4}$.

The slope is $\frac{3}{4}$.

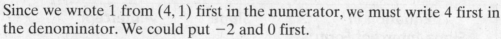

You could also find the slope from just the coordinates $(0, -2)$ and $(4, 1)$.

slope $= \frac{\text{difference in } y-\text{coordinates}}{\text{difference in } x-\text{coordinates}} = \frac{1 - (-2)}{4 - 0} = \frac{3}{4}$

Since we wrote 1 from $(4, 1)$ first in the numerator, we must write 4 first in the denominator. We could put -2 and 0 first.

slope $= \frac{-2 - 1}{0 - 4} = \frac{-3}{-4} = \frac{3}{4}$

Find the slope of each line.

1.  _____

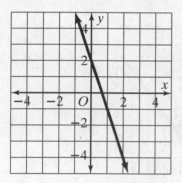

2. _____

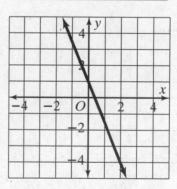

Find the slope of the line through each pair of points.

3. $A(8, 2), B(4, 1)$

4. $L(-3, 6), M(5, -1)$

5. $J(6, -2), K(4, 3)$

6. $P(3, -1), Q(5, 5)$

7. $S(4, 1), T(-9, 1)$

8. $G(-2, -7), H(-2, 0)$

Practice 8-3 Slope and y-intercept

Find the slope of the line through each pair of points.

1. $A(1, 1), B(6, 3)$

2. $J(-4, 6), K(-4, 2)$

_____

_____

3. $P(3, -7), Q(-1, -7)$

4. $M(7, 2), N(-1, 3)$

_____

_____

Complete the table.

Equation	Equation in Slope-Intercept Form	Slope	y-intercept
5. $5x - y = 6$			
6. $7x + 2y = 10$			

Find the slope of each line.

7. _____

8. _____

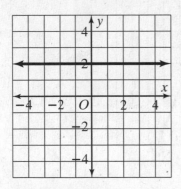

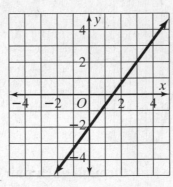

Graph each equation.

9. $y = -2x + 3$

10. $y = \frac{1}{3}x - 1$

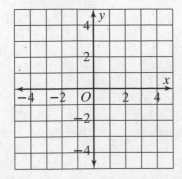

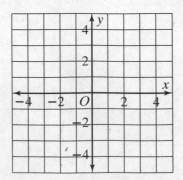

Reteaching 8-4 Writing Rules for Linear Functions

Write a rule for the function.

x	$f(x)$
-2	-12
0	-2
2	8
4	18

As the x values increase by 2, the $f(x)$ values increase by 10. So $m = \frac{10}{2} = 5$. When $x = 0$, $f(x) = -2$. So $b = -2$. Substitute $m = 5$ and $b = -2$ into $f(x) = mx + b$.
$f(x) = 5x + (-2)$
$f(x) = 5x - 2$

Write a rule for each function.

1. _____

x	$f(x)$
-1	-7
0	0
1	7
2	14

2. _____

x	$f(x)$
-9	-17
0	-8
9	1
18	10

3. _____

x	$f(x)$
0	9
2	5
4	1
6	-3

4. _____

x	$f(x)$
-6	7
-3	8
0	9
3	10

5. _____

x	$f(x)$
-4	-6
0	-7
4	-8
8	-9

6. _____

x	$f(x)$
-12	-83
-6	-47
0	-11
6	25

Practice 8-4 *Writing Rules for Linear Functions*

Write a rule for each function.

1. _____

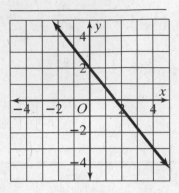

2. _____

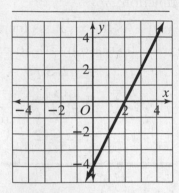

3. _____

x	$f(x)$
−3	18
−1	6
1	−6
3	−18

4. _____

x	$f(x)$
5	−2
7	0
9	2
11	4

5. _____

x	$f(x)$
−3	−17
−1	−11
1	−5
3	1

6. _____

x	$f(x)$
−4	4
0	6
2	7
4	8

Write a function rule to describe each situation.

7. The number of pounds $p(z)$ as a function of the number of ounces z.

_____

8. The selling price $s(c)$ after a 45% markup of an item as a function of the stores' cost c.

_____

9. The total number of miles $m(r)$ covered when you walk 7 miles before lunch, and you walk for 2 hours at r mi/hr after lunch.

_____

Name _____ Class _____ Date _____

Reteaching 8-5 *Scatter Plots*

Make a (U.S. Open wins, Wimbledon wins) scatter plot of the data in the table. Is there a *positive correlation*, a *negative correlation*, or *no correlation* between the two sets of data?

Player	U.S. Open	Wimble-don	French Open	Aust. Open
Andre Agassi	1	1	0	1
Jimmy Conners	5	2	0	1
Chris Evert	6	3	7	2
Steffie Graf	5	7	5	4
John McEnroe	4	3	0	0
Martina Navratilova	4	9	2	3
Pete Sampras	4	4	0	2
Monica Seles	2	0	3	4

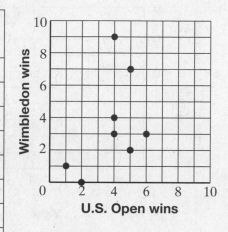

Plot each (U.S. Open wins, Wimbledon wins) ordered pair.

There does not seem to be a trend in the data. As the number of U.S. Open wins increase, the number of Wimbledon wins does not seem to increase or decrease. Thus, there is no correlation.

---

1. Make a (U.S. Open wins, French Open wins) scatter plot using the data in the table above.

2. Make a (Wimbledon wins, Australian Open wins) scatter plot using the data in the table above.

Is there a *positive correlation*, a *negative correlation*, or *no correlation* between the data sets in each scatter plot?

3. (U.S. Open wins, French Open wins) _____

4. (Wimbledon wins, Australian Open wins) _____

Practice 8-5 Scatter Plots

Use the data in the table.

1. Make a (year, units of CDs) scatter plot.

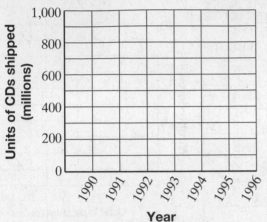

Sales of Recorded Music			
Year	Millions of Units Shipped		
	CDs	Cassettes	LPs
1990	287	442	12
1991	333	360	5
1992	408	366	2
1993	495	340	1
1994	662	345	2
1995	723	273	2
1996	779	225	3

2. Make a (year, units of cassettes) scatter plot.

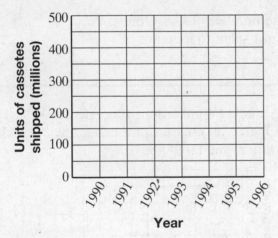

3. Make a (year, units of LPs) scatter plot.

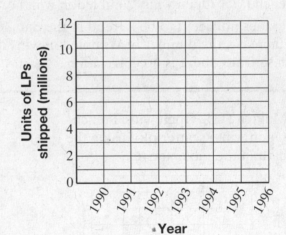

Is there a *positive correlation*, a *negative correlation*, or *no correlation* between the data sets in each scatter plot?

4. (year, units of CDs) scatter plot _____

5. (year, units of cassettes) scatter plot _____

6. (year, units of LPs) scatter plot _____

Reteaching 8-6 Solve by Graphing

The driver of a car slows to a stop. After 3 seconds the car is traveling 41 mi/h. After 5 seconds it is traveling 30 mi/h and after 8 seconds it is traveling 12 mi/h.

Braking Rates

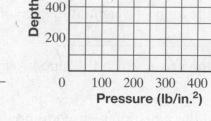

  a. Make a scatter plot of the data and draw a trend line. Plot the points (3, 41), (5, 30) and (8, 12). Draw a line through (5, 30) and (8, 12).

  b. About how fast was the car moving when the driver first applied the brakes?
    When the time was 0, the speed was about 60. So the driver was moving about 60 mi/h.

  c. Write an equation for your trend line.
    The y-intercept, b, is about 60. You can use the points (5, 30) and (8, 12) to find the slope.
    $$m = \frac{\text{difference in } y\text{-values}}{\text{difference in } x\text{-values}} = \frac{12 - 30}{8 - 5} = \frac{-18}{3} = -6$$
    Substitute $m = -6$ and $b = 60$ into $y = mx + b$.
    $y = mx + b$
    $y = -6x + 60$

  d. Use your equation to find about how long it took for the car to stop.
    When the car stops, the speed, y, is zero.
    $y = -6x + 60$
    $0 = -6x + 60$
    $6x = 60$
    $x = 10$
    It took the car about 10 seconds to stop.

The water pressure at a depth of 100 ft in the ocean is 45 lb/in.^{2}. At a depth of 500 ft the pressure is 225 lb/in.^{2}.

Water Pressure

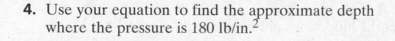

  1. Make a (pressure, depth) scatter plot of the data.

  2. Draw a trend line.

  3. Write an equation for your trend line.

  _____

  4. Use your equation to find the approximate depth where the pressure is 180 lb/in.^{2}

  _____

  5. Use you equation to find the approximate pressure at a depth of 800 ft.

  _____

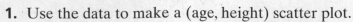

Practice 8-6 *Solve by Graphing*

A giraffe was 1 ft tall at birth, 7 ft tall at the age of 4, and $11\frac{1}{2}$ ft tall at the age of 7.

1. Use the data to make a (age, height) scatter plot.

2. Draw a trend line.

3. Write an equation for your trend line in slope-intercept form.

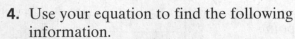

4. Use your equation to find the following information.

a. the giraffe's height at the age of 5

b. the age at which the giraffe was 16 ft tall

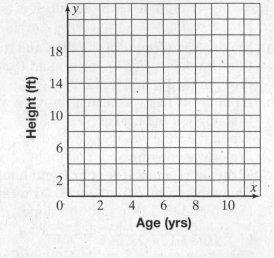

Giraffe Height

A hippopotamus weighed 700 lb at the age of 1 and 1,900 lb at the age of 3, and 2,500 lb at the age of 4.

5. Use the data to make a (age, weight) scatter plot.

6. Draw a trend line.

7. Write an equation for your trend line.

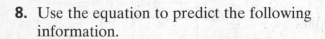

8. Use the equation to predict the following information.

a. the hippo's weight at the age of 8

b. the age at which the hippo weighed 7,900 lb

9. Can this equation be used to predict the hippo's weight at any age? Explain.

_____

_____

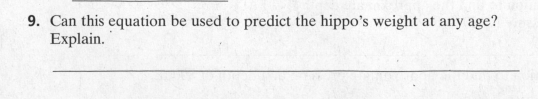

Hippopotamus Weight

Reteaching 8-7 Solving Systems of Linear Equations

Solve the system. Check your solution.

$$y = 2x - 5$$
$$x - y = 4$$

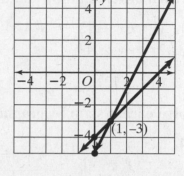

Graph $y = 2x - 5$.
Solve $x - y = 4$, for y.

$x - y = 4$	
$x - y + y = 4 + y$	Add y to each side.
$x = 4 + y$	Simplify.
$x - 4 = 4 + y - 4$	Subtract 4 from each side.
$x - 4 = y$	Simplify.

Graph $y = x - 4$.
The lines intersect at $(1, -3)$. This is the solution to the system.

Check by substituting 1 for x and -3 for y in each equation.

$y = 2x - 5$	$x - y = 4$
$-3 = 2(1) - 5$	$1 - (-3) = 4$
$-3 = 2 - 5$	$1 + 3 = 4$
$-3 = -3$	$4 = 4$

Both are true. The solution is correct.

Solve each system by graphing. Check your solution.

1. $3x + y = -1$
$x - y = -3$

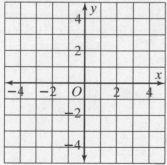

Solution: _____

2. $y = 4x + 5$
$x - 2y = 4$

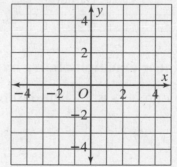

Solution: _____

Practice 8-7 Solving Systems of Linear Equations

Is each ordered pair a solution of the given system? Write *yes* or *no*.

1. $y = 6x + 12$
$2x - y = 4$

$(-4, -12)$ _____

2. $y = -3x$
$x = 4y + \frac{1}{2}$

$\left(-\frac{1}{2}, \frac{3}{2}\right)$ _____

3. $x + 2y = 2$
$2x + 5y = 2$

$(6, -2)$ _____

Solve each system by graphing. Check your solution.

4. $x + y = 3$
$x - y = -1$
Solution:

_____

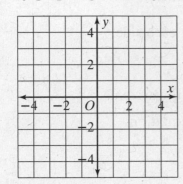

5. $2x + y = 1$
$x - 2y = 3$
Solution:

_____

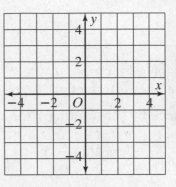

6. $y + 2 = 0$
$2x + y = 0$
Solution:

_____

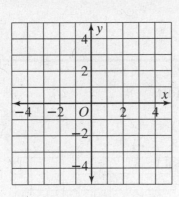

7. $3x + 2y = -6$
$x + 3y = -2$
Solution:

_____

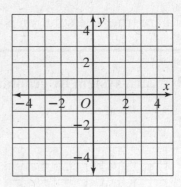

Write a system of linear equations. Solve by graphing.

8. The sum of two numbers is 3. Their difference is 1. Find the numbers.

_____

_____

_____

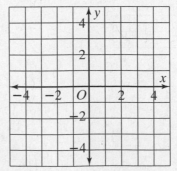

Reteaching 8-8 Graphing Linear Inequalities

Graph $y < 2x - 1$.

Graph the boundary line $y = 2x - 1$. The y-intercept is -1 and the slope is 2. Since the inequality is $<$, the boundary line should be dashed.

Try a test point. The origin $(0, 0)$ is usually easy to use.

$$y < 2x - 1$$
$$0 \overset{?}{<} 2(0) - 1$$
$$0 \overset{?}{<} -1 \qquad \text{No}$$

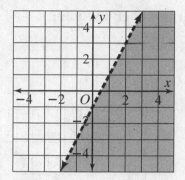

$(0, 0)$ is not in the solution of $y < 2x - 1$. Shade the side of the boundary line *not* containing the origin.

Tell whether the boundary line of the graph of each inequality is *solid* or *dashed*.

1. $4x - 5y \geq 3$

_____

2. $y < \frac{2}{3}x + 2$

_____

3. $2x \gtrless 3 - 2y$

_____

4. $y \leq -5$

_____

5. $-x + 2y > -3$

_____

6. $8 \leq 5y - 3x$

_____

Tell whether the region containing the origin would be shaded in the graph of each inequality. Write *yes* or *no*.

7. $4x - 5y \geq 3$

_____

8. $y < \frac{2}{3}x + 2$

_____

9. $2x > 3 - 2y$

_____

10. $y \leq -5$

_____

11. $-x + 2y > -3$

_____

12. $8 \leq 5y - 3x$

_____

13. $4x < y$

_____

14. $\frac{3}{4}x > 2y$

_____

Practice 8-8 Graphing Linear Inequalities

Graph each inequality.

1. $y < x$

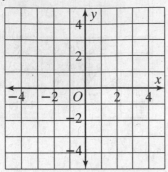

2. $x + y \leq 2$

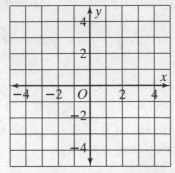

3. $x + 2y \geq 4$

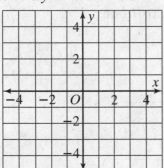

4. $x > -2$

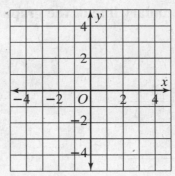

Solve each system by graphing.

5. $y \geq -x - 2$
$x - 2y < 4$

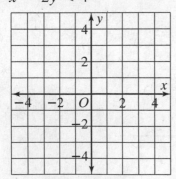

6. $x + y < 3$
$y \geq 3x - 2$

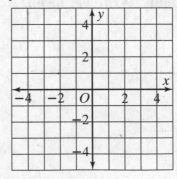

7. Is the origin a solution to the system in Exercise 5? _____

8. Is $(4, 0)$ a solution to the system in Exercise 5? _____

9. Is $(1, 0)$ a solution to the system in Exercise 6? _____

10. Is $(-1, 0)$ a solution to the system in Exercise 6? _____

Reteaching 9-1 Introduction to Geometry: Points, Lines, and Planes

Name all points, segments, lines, and rays shown.

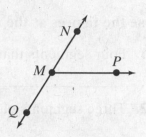

Points are represented with a single capital letter. The points shown are $M, N, Q,$ and $P.$

A segment has two endpoints. We write the segment with endpoints M and N as either $\overline{MN}$ or $\overline{NM}$. One way to list the segments shown is: $\overline{MN}, \overline{MP}, \overline{MQ}, \overline{NQ}$.

Lines are infinite. We can name them with any two points. One line in the figure is $\overleftrightarrow{MN}$. The arrows indicate the line extends in each direction without end. Other names for the same line are $\overleftrightarrow{NM}, \overleftrightarrow{NQ}, \overleftrightarrow{QN}, \overleftrightarrow{MQ},$ and $\overleftrightarrow{QM}$.

A ray has one endpoint and extends without end in one direction. The endpoint is named first. Thus, $\overrightarrow{MQ}$ and $\overrightarrow{QM}$ are not the same ray. However, $\overrightarrow{QM}$ and $\overrightarrow{QN}$ are the same ray. After the endpoint, we can use any other point on the line to name the ray. The rays shown are: $\overrightarrow{MQ}, \overrightarrow{MN}, \overrightarrow{MP}, \overrightarrow{NM}, \overrightarrow{QM}$.

Use the figure below. Name each of the following.

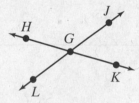

1. all points shown

   _____

2. all rays shown

   _____

3. all names for $\overleftrightarrow{JL}$

   _____

4. all segments on $\overleftrightarrow{HK}$

   _____

Practice 9-1 Introduction to Geometry: Points, Lines, and Planes

Use the figures at the right. Name each of the following.

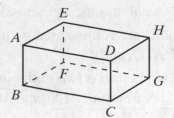

1. Four segments that intersect $\overline{AB}$.

_____

2. Three segments parallel to $\overline{AB}$.

_____

3. Four segments skew to $\overline{AB}$.

_____

Use the figure at the right. Find each of the following.

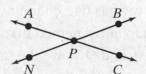

4. all points shown

_____

5. all segments shown

_____

6. five different rays

_____

7. all lines shown

_____

8. all names for $\overleftrightarrow{NB}$

_____

Write an equation. Then find the length of each segment.

9.

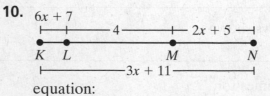

equation:

_____

$n =$ _____

$AB =$ _____ $AC =$

10.

equation:

_____

$x =$ _____

$MN =$ _____ $KN =$ _____

▬▬Reteaching 9-2 Angle Relationships and Parallel Lines

Find the measures of ∠1 and ∠2. Given: $r \parallel s$.
Write an equation and solve for x.

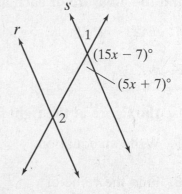

$(5x + 7) + (15x - 7) = 180$	These angles are supplementary.
$5x + 15x + 7 - 7 = 180$	Simplify.
$20x = 180$	Simplify.
$\frac{20x}{20} = \frac{180}{20}$	Divide each side by 20.
$x = 9$	Simplify.

Find the measure of the angle marked $(5x + 7)°$ by
substituting $x = 9$.

$$5x + 7 = 5(9) + 7 = 45 + 7 = 52$$

Since this angle and ∠1 are vertical, they have the same measure.
Thus, $m\angle 1 = 52°$.

We can find the measure of ∠2 several ways. The angle marked $(15x - 7)°$
and ∠2 are corresponding angles, so they have the same measure. We can
find this measure by substituting $x = 9$ into $15x - 7$ or by realizing that this
angle and ∠1 are supplementary.

$180 - 52 = 128$

$15x - 7 = 15(9) - 7 = 135 - 7 = 128$

Either way, $m\angle 2 = 128°$.

Use the figure at the right.

Given: $p \parallel q$.

1. Write an equation.

   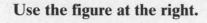

2. Find the value of x.

   $x =$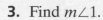

3. Find $m\angle 1$.

   $m\angle 1 =$ _____

4. Find $m\angle 2$.

   $m\angle 2 =$ _____

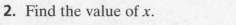

Practice 9-2 Angle Relationships and Parallel Lines

Find the measure of each angle in the figure at the right.

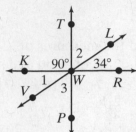

1. $m\angle 1$

2. $m\angle 2$

3. $m\angle 3$

4. $m\angle VWR$

Use the figure at the right for Exercises 5-8.

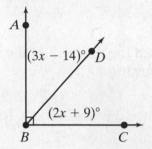

5. Write an equation. _____

6. Find the value of x. _____

7. Find $m\angle ABD$. _____

8. Find $m\angle DBC$. _____

Use the figure at the right for Exercises 9-12.

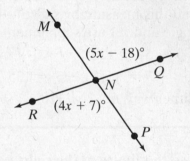

9. Write an equation. _____

10. Find the value of x. _____

11. Find $m\angle MNQ$. _____

12. Find $m\angle MNR$. _____

In each figure, find the measures of $\angle 1$ and $\angle 2$.

13. Given $p \parallel q$.

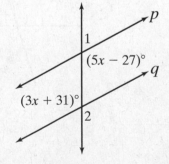

14. Given $a \parallel b$.

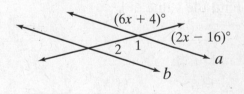

$m\angle 1 =$ $m\angle 2 =$ $m\angle 1 =$ $m\angle 2 =$

15. Find a pair of complementary angles such that the difference of their measures is 12°.

_____

Reteaching 9-3 *Classifying Polygons*

Classify the triangle below by its sides and angles.

First, look at the sides. Two sides are congruent and the third side is not. The triangle is isosceles. Next, look at the angles. All three angles are acute.

The triangle is an acute isosceles triangle.

Judging by appearances, classify each triangle by its sides and angles.

1.

_____

2.

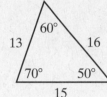

_____

3.

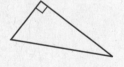

_____

4.

_____

Give all names for each quadrilateral.

5.

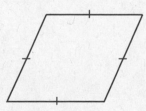

_____

_____

6.

_____

_____

Practice 9-3 *Classifying Polygons*

Name all quadrilaterals that have each of the named properties.

1. four 90° angles

_____

2. opposite sides congruent and parallel

_____

3. at least one pair of parallel sides

_____

_____

Judging by appearances, classify each triangle by its sides and angles.

4.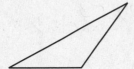

_____

5.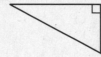

_____

6.

9   9

9

_____

7.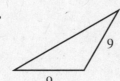

9

9

_____

Write a formula to find the perimeter of each figure. Use the formula to find the perimeter.

8. a regular dodecagon (12-gon); one side is 9.25 cm

P = _____   P = _____

9. a rhombus; one side is $1\frac{3}{4}$ yd

P = _____   P = _____

10. a parallelogram; the sides are 10.4 m and 5.6 m

P = _____   P = _____

Reteaching 9-4 Draw a Diagram

Solve by drawing a diagram.

Kara and Karl are twins with the same tastes. They like pizza more than tacos, but less than steak. They like mashed potatoes more than tacos, but less than hamburgers. They like hamburgers more than pizza, but less than steak. Which of these foods do they like the most?

Let p = pizza, t = tacos, s = steak, m = mashed potatoes, and h = hamburgers.

Draw a diagram with 5 blanks. Since Kara and Karl like pizza more than tacos, but less than steak, start by putting s, p, and t in the first 3 blanks.

_____ s _____   _____ p _____   _____ t _____   _____   _____

They like mashed potatoes more than tacos, but less than hamburgers. This moves tacos down. Tentatively, we have:

_____ s _____   _____ p _____   _____ h _____   _____ m _____   _____ t _____

They like hamburgers more than pizza but less than steak.

_____ s _____   _____ h _____   _____ p _____   _____ m _____   _____ t _____

We still cannot be sure if they like pizza more or less than mashed potatoes, but that is not important for answering the question. Kara and Karl like steak the most.

Solve by drawing a diagram.

1. Mindy is taller than Olga, but shorter than Thomas. Thomas is taller than Sven, but shorter than Parth. Sven is taller than Olga, but shorter than Mindy. Who's the tallest?

   _____ _____ _____ _____ _____ _____ _____ _____ _____ _____

   _____ _____ _____ _____ _____ _____ _____ _____ _____ _____

   _____ _____ _____ _____ _____ _____ _____ _____ _____ _____

2. How many segments can you draw between pairs of points in the figure at the right?

   _____

Name _____ Class _____ Date _____

■ *Practice 9-4* Draw a Diagram

Solve by drawing a diagram.

1. How many diagonals does a quadrilateral have?

   _____

2. Which quadrilaterals always have congruent diagonals?

   _____

3. Find a formula for the number of diagonals *d* in a polygon with *n* sides.
   Complete the table to help you. Look for a pattern.

Figure	Number of sides	Number of vertices	Number of diagonals from each vertex	Total number of diagonals
triangle	3			
quadrilateral	4			
pentagon	5			
hexagon	6			
octagon	8			
n-gon	*n*			

   d = _____

4. One day in the lunch line, Maurice was ahead of Aquia and behind
   Rochelle. Rochelle was ahead of Shequille and behind Whitney.
   Shequille was ahead of Maurice. Who was last?

   _____

5. A mail carrier leaves the post office at 10:00 A.M. and travels 4 miles
   south, then 7 miles east, then 5 miles south, then 10 miles west, and 9
   miles north. At the end of her route, how far and in which direction is
   the mail carrier from the post office?

   _____

Reteaching 9-5 Congruence

List the congruent corresponding parts of the pair of triangles. Write a congruence statement for the triangles.

$\angle ACB \cong \angle ACD$ because both are right angles.

$\overline{BC} \cong \overline{DC}$ because they are marked.

$\overline{AC} \cong \overline{AC}$ because these are the same segment in each triangle.

Thus, $\triangle ABC \cong \triangle ADC$ by SAS (side-angle-side).

The vertices must be listed in the same order that they correspond.

$A \leftrightarrow A$

$B \leftrightarrow D$

$C \leftrightarrow C$

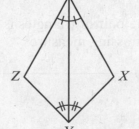

List the congruent corresponding parts of each pair of triangles. Write a congruence statement for the triangles.

1. _____

_____

_____

_____ by _____

2. _____

_____

_____

_____ by _____

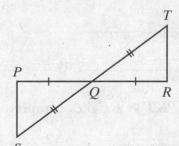

3. _____

_____

_____

_____ by _____

Practice 9-5 Congruence

Given that $\triangle GHM \cong \triangle RSA$, **complete the following.**

1. $\overline{GH} \cong$ _____

2. $\overline{AS} \cong$ _____

3. $\angle S \cong$ _____

4. $\angle M \cong$ _____

5. $\overline{AR} \cong$ _____

6. $\angle R \cong$ _____

7. $m\angle A =$ _____

8. $m\angle G =$ _____

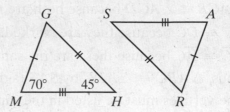

List the congruent corresponding parts of each pair of triangles. Write a congruence statement for the triangles.

9. _____

   _____

   _____

   _____ by _____

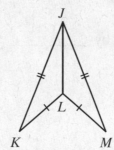

10. _____

   _____

   _____

   _____ by _____

Given that $HPKT \cong BEWL$, **complete the following.**

11. $\overline{PK} \cong$ _____

12. $\angle L \cong$ _____

13. $\angle KPH \cong$ _____

14. $\overline{LB} \cong$ _____

15. $\overline{EB} \cong$ _____

16. $\angle PHT \cong$ _____

17. Explain why the pair of triangles is congruent.
    Then, find the missing measures.

    _____

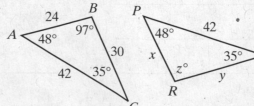

Reteaching 9-6 Circles

Find the measures of the central angles that you would draw to represent each percent in a circle graph. Round to the nearest degree.

Employment Distribution in California				
Service	Trade	Manufacturing	Government	Other
31%	23%	15%	17%	14%

You can use proportions to find the measures of the central angles. You also can use equations.

What is 31% of 360?
$n = (0.31)(360)$
$n \approx 112°$

What is 23% of 360?
$n = (0.23)(360)$
$n \approx 83°$

What is 15% of 360?
$n = (0.15)(360)$
$n = 54°$

What is 17% of 360?
$n = (0.17)(360)$
$n \approx 61°$

What is 14% of 360?
$n = (0.14)(360)$
$n \approx 50°$

Find the measures of the central angle that you would draw to represent each percent in a circle graph. Round to the nearest degree.

Measure of central angle

	Employment Distribution in Texas	
1.	Service	27%
2.	Trade	24%
3.	Manufacturing	13%
4.	Government	18%
5.	Other	18%

1. _____
2. _____
3. _____
4. _____
5. _____

Practice 9-6 Circles

Find the measures of the central angles that you would draw to represent each percent in a circle graph. Round to the nearest degree.

	Voter Preference for Senator		Central Angle
1.	Peterson	40%	
2.	Washington	30%	
3.	Gomez	15%	
4.	Thomson	10%	
5.	Miller	5%	

6. Draw a circle graph for the data on voter preference.

Voter Preference for Senator

7. The total number of voters surveyed was 5,000. How many voters preferred Gomez?

Find the circumference of each circle with the given radius or diameter. Use 3.14 for π.

8. $d = 25.8$ m

$C =$ _____

9. $r = 9.1$ cm

$C =$ _____

10. $r = 0.28$ km

$C =$ _____

11. $d = 14$ ft

$C =$ _____

12. $d = 5$ in.

$C =$ _____

13. $r = \frac{7}{8}$ in.

$C =$ _____

Reteaching 9-7 Constructions

Construct an angle with a measure of 112.5°. We know how to construct a right angle. One half of 90 is 45, one half of 45 is 22.5, and $90 + 22.5 = 112.5$.

First draw a segment, $\overline{TU}$ and construct its perpendicular bisector, $\overleftrightarrow{JK}$.

Then bisect $\angle USJ$.
Then bisect $\angle LSJ$.
$m\angle RST = 112.5°$

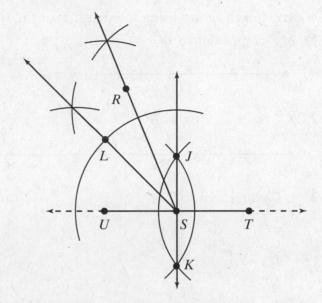

Construct each figure using the diagram on the right.

1. $\angle BCD$ congruent to $\angle A$

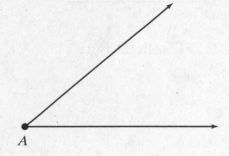

C •————————————————➤

2. $\angle EFG$ with measure half $\angle A$

F •————————————————➤

3. $\angle HJK$ with measure 1.5 times $\angle A$

J •————————————————➤

Practice 9-7 Constructions

Construct each figure using the diagram at the right.

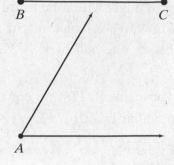

1. $\overline{MP}$ congruent to $\overline{BC}$

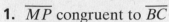

2. $\overline{JK}$ twice as long as $\overline{BC}$

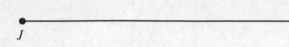

3. $\angle D$ congruent to $\angle A$

4. $\angle PQR$ half the measure of $\angle A$

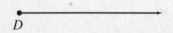

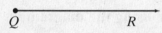

5. $\angle STU$ with measure 135°

6. $\overline{EF}$ half as long as $\overline{BC}$

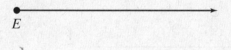

7. Construct $\triangle WXY$ so that $\angle W$ is congruent to $\angle A$, $\overline{WY}$ is congruent to $\overline{BC}$, and $\angle Y$ is half the measure of $\angle A$.

8. What seems to be true about $\angle X$ in $\triangle WXY$ you constructed?

_____

Reteaching 9-8 Translations

Write a rule to describe the translation.
Point A has coordinates $(-2, 3)$. It's image A' has coordinates $(-1, -2)$. To move from A to A' on the graph, we go right one unit $(+1)$ and down 5 units (-5). So the rule is $(x, y) \rightarrow (x + 1, y - 5)$. We could also subtract coordinates:
x: $-1 - (-2) = -1 + 2 = 1$
y: $-2 - 3 = -2 + (-3) = -5$

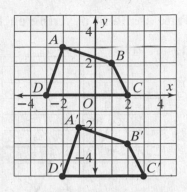

Write a rule to describe each translation.

1. $(x, y) \rightarrow$ _____

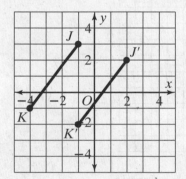

2. $(x, y) \rightarrow$ _____

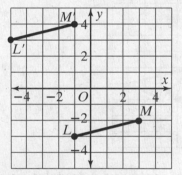

3. $(x, y) \rightarrow$ _____

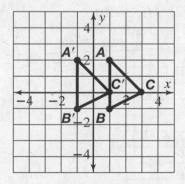

4. $(x, y) \rightarrow$ _____

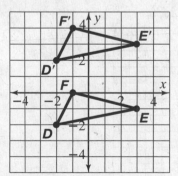

5. The translation that takes $A(8, -6)$ to $A'(9, -3)$

   $(x, y) \rightarrow$ _____

6. The translation that takes $B(2, -10)$ to $B'(-7, -12)$

   $(x, y) \rightarrow$ _____

Practice 9-8 Translations

Write a rule to describe each translation.

1. $(x, y) \rightarrow$ _____

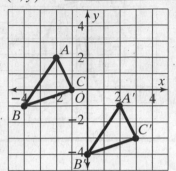

2. $(x, y) \rightarrow$ _____

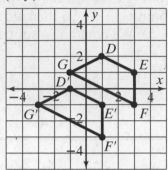

3. $(x, y) \rightarrow$ _____

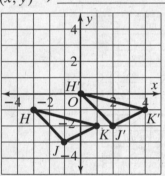

4. $(x, y) \rightarrow$ _____

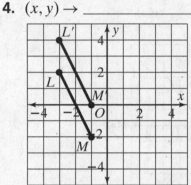

The vertices of a triangle and a translation are given. Graph each triangle and its image.

5. $G(-4, 4), H(-2, 3),$
$J(-3, 0);$ right 5 and down 2

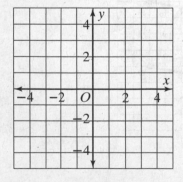

6. $K(0, -1), L(4, 2), M(3, -3);$
left 4 units and up 3 units

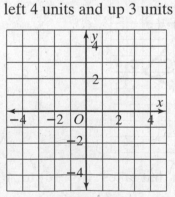

A point and its image after a translation are given. Write a rule to describe the translation.

7. $A(9, -4), A'(2, -1)$ $(x, y) \rightarrow$ _____

8. $B(-3, 5), B'(-5, -3)$ $(x, y) \rightarrow$ _____

Name _____ Class _____ Date _____

Reteaching 9-9 Symmetry and Reflections

Graph the polygon's image after a reflection over the line $x = 1$.
Name the coordinates of the image.

Graph $x = 1$.

Point A is 1 unit left of $x = 1$.

Plot A' with the same y-coordinate and 1 unit right of $x = 1$.

Point B is 3 units left of $x = 1$.

Plot B' 3 units right of $x = 1$.

Point C is 2 units left of $x = 1$.

Plot C' 2 units right of $x = 1$.

Read the coordinates.

$A'(2, 2), B'(4, 1), C'(3, -2)$

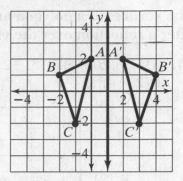

Graph each polygon's image after a reflection over the given line. Name the coordinates of the image.

1. $x = 2$

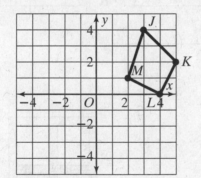

J' _____ K' _____

L' _____ M' _____

2. $y = 1$

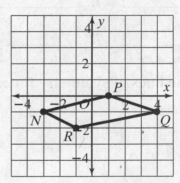

N' _____ P' _____

Q' _____ R' _____

3. $y = -1$

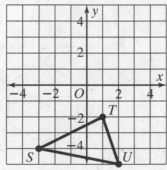

S' _____ T' _____

U' _____

4. $x = -3$

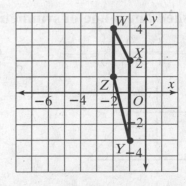

W' _____ X' _____

Y' _____ Z' _____

Practice 9-9 *Symmetry and Reflections*

The vertices of a polygon are listed. Graph each polygon and its image after a reflection over the given line. Name the coordinates of the image.

1. $A(1, 3), B(4, 1), C(3, -2),$
$D(2, -4); x = 0$

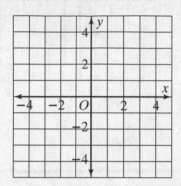

2. $J(-2, 1), K(1, 3), L(4, 2);$
$y = -1$

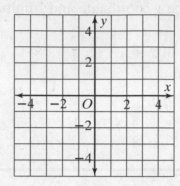

A' _____ B' _____

C' _____ D' _____

J' _____ K' _____

L' _____

Draw all the lines of symmetry for each figure.

3.

4.

5.

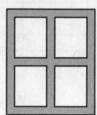

Is the dashed line a line of symmetry? Write yes or no.

6. _____

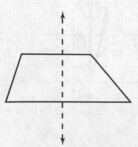

7. _____

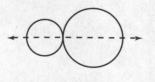

8. _____

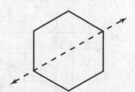

Reteaching 9-10 Rotations

$\triangle PQR$ has vertices $P(1, 4)$, $Q(2, 1)$ and $R(4, 2)$. Graph the triangle and its image after a rotation of (a) 90° and (b) 180° about the origin.

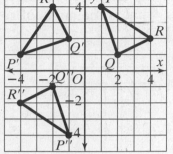

Graph $\triangle PQR$. Trace it onto tracing paper and label the vertices. Also trace the axes. Place your pencil at the origin. Turn the paper counterclockwise until the y-axis on the tracing paper is on top of the x-axis of the graph. Mark the position of each vertex by pressing through the paper. Connect the vertices of the rotated triangle and label them P', Q', and R'. The coordinates are $P'(-4, 1)$, $Q'(-1, 2)$, and $R'(-2, 4)$. Put your tracing paper back in its original position. Now turn it until +5 on the tracing paper x-axis is by −5 on the graph's x-axis. Mark the vertices, connect them, and label them P'', Q'', and R''. The coordinates are $P''(-1, -4)$, $Q''(-2, -1)$, and $R''(-4, -2)$.

---

1. The coordinates of $\triangle PQR$, its image after a 90° rotation $\triangle P'Q'R'$, and its image after a 180° rotation $\triangle P''Q''R''$ are listed in the table. Look for a pattern. What is the result on any point (x, y) of (a) a 90° rotation, (b) an 180° rotation? Complete the table.

Point	Image	
	90° Rotation	180° Rotation
$P(1, 4)$	$P'(-4, 1)$	$P''(-1, -4)$
$Q(2, 1)$	$Q'(-1, 2)$	$Q''(-2, -1)$
$R(4, 2)$	$R'(-2, 4)$	$R''(-4, -2)$
(x, y)		

The vertices of a triangle are given. Graph each triangle and its image after a rotation of (a) 90° and (b) 180° about the origin. Name the coordinates of the vertices of the images. Use tracing paper or the pattern you found.

2. $J(1, 3), K(3, 3), L(1, 0)$

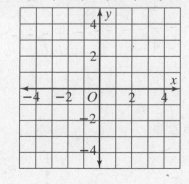

     90°   180°

J' _____ J'' _____

K' _____ K'' _____

L' _____ L'' _____

3. $W(0, 4), Y(1, 2), Z(-1, 1)$

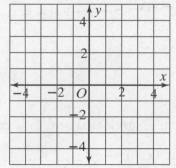

     90°   180°

W' _____ W'' _____

Y' _____ Y'' _____

Z' _____ Z'' _____

Practice 9-10 Rotations

Judging from appearances, does each figure have rotational symmetry? If yes, what is the angle of rotation?

1. _____

2. _____

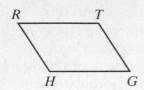

3. _____

The vertices of a triangle are given. Graph each triangle and its image after a rotation of (a) 90° and (b) 180° about the origin. Name the coordinates of the vertices of the images.

4. $A(1, 4), B(1, 1), C(4, 2)$

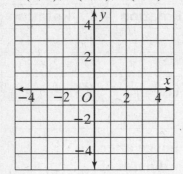

    90°   180°

5. $S(2, 3), T(-2, 4), U(-4, 2)$

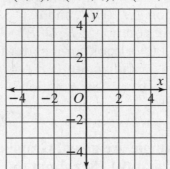

    90°   180°

A' _____ A'' _____ S' _____ S'' _____

B' _____ B'' _____ T' _____ T'' _____

C' _____ C'' _____ U' _____ U'' _____

Look for a pattern in Exercises 4 and 5 to complete the following.

6. In a 90° rotation, $(x, y) \rightarrow$ _____

7. In a 180° rotation, $(x, y) \rightarrow$ _____

Name _____ Class _____ Date _____

Reteaching 10-1 Area: Parallelograms

Draw the parallelogram with vertices $A(-2, 4)$, $B(1, 4)$, $C(0, -2)$, and $D(-3, -2)$. Find its area.

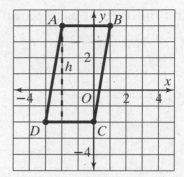

Plot the four points and connect them to form the parallelogram. To find the area, find the length of a base and the height to that base. Any one of the four sides could be used as the base. The easiest side to use is $\overline{DC}$.

Count in the figure.

$DC = 3$ units, so $b = 3$.

Draw the height as a dashed line from A, perpendicular to $\overline{DC}$. Count in the figure, $h = 6$.

So $A = bh = 3(6) = 18$ units^2.

The vertices of a parallelogram are given. Draw each parallelogram. Find its area.

1. $E(-1, 2), F(3, 2), G(1, 1), H(-3, 1)$

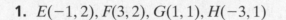

2. $M(-2, 1), N(2, 1), Q(-3, -2), P(1, -2)$

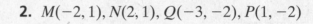

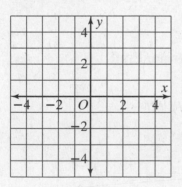

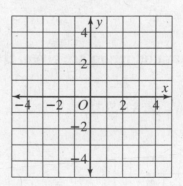

3. $R(1, 3), S(3, 3), U(-1, -4), T(1, -4)$

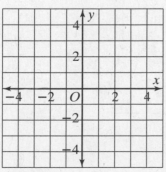

4. $V(-3, -1), W(5, -1), Y(-4, -3),$ $X(4, -3)$

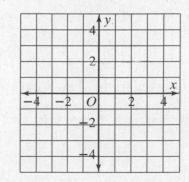

Name _____ Class _____ Date _____

Find the area of each parallelogram.

1.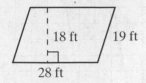
18 ft 19 ft
28 ft

2.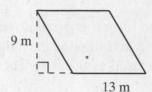
9 m
13 m

3.
5 m
50 cm

_____   _____   _____

Find the area of each shaded region. Assume that all angles that appear to be right angles are right angles.

4.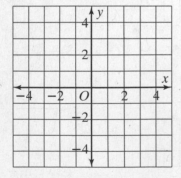
80 ft
50 ft
35 ft
70 ft
25 ft
20 ft

5.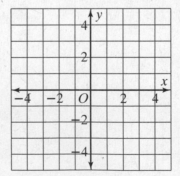
65 m
30 m   30 m
45 m
15 m   15 m
10 m   10 m

_____   _____

The vertices of a parallelogram are given. Draw each parallelogram. Find its area.

6. $P(1, 1), Q(3, 1), R(2, 4), S(4, 4)$

7. $J(-3, 2), K(1, 2), M(-1, -3), L(3, -3)$

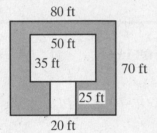

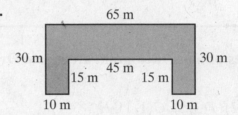

8. The perimeter of a square is 72 in. What is its area?

_____

Name _____ Class _____ Date _____

Reteaching 10-2 Area: Triangles and Trapezoids

Find the area of the trapezoid.

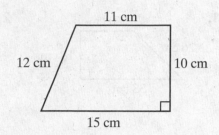

The formula for the area A of a trapezoid is $A = \frac{1}{2}h(b_1 + b_2)$, where h is the height and b_1 and b_2 are the lengths of the bases. The bases are the two sides that are parallel. So, the bases of the trapezoid in the figure have lengths 15 cm and 11 cm. Let $b_1 = 15$ and $b_2 = 11$. The height is the perpendicular distance between the bases. Since the trapezoid has right angles, the height is the side with length 10 cm. So, $h = 10$.

$$A = \tfrac{1}{2}h(b_1 + b_2)$$

$A = \frac{1}{2} \cdot 10(15 + 11)$ Substitute 10 for h, 15 for b_1, and 11 for b_2.

$A = \frac{1}{2} \cdot 10(26)$ Simplify, using the order of operations.

$A = 130$ Multiply.

So, the area of the trapezoid is 130 cm^2.

Find the area of each trapezoid.

1.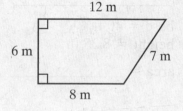

2.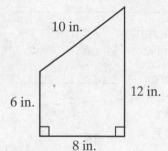

3.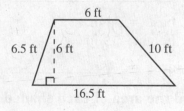

_____   _____   _____

4. $b_1 = 25$ cm
$b_2 = 18$ cm
$h = 12$ cm

5. $b_1 = 4$ ft
$b_2 = 7$ ft
$h = 5$ ft

6. $b_1 = 85$ mm
$b_2 = 73$ mm
$h = 48$ mm

_____   _____   _____

7. $b_1 = 1.5$ in.
$b_2 = 3.5$ in.
$h = 4.5$ in.

8. $b_1 = 50$ m
$b_2 = 60$ m
$h = 40$ m

9. $b_1 = 12.4$ km
$b_2 = 8.8$ km
$h = 9$ km

_____   _____   _____

Practice 10-2 Area: Triangles and Trapezoids

Find the area of each trapezoid.

1.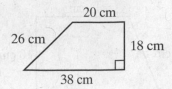
20 cm
26 cm   18 cm
38 cm

_____

2.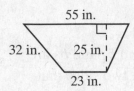
55 in.
32 in.   25 in.
23 in.

_____

3.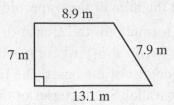
8.9 m
7 m   7.9 m
13.1 m

_____

4. base$_1$ = 13 in.
base$_2$ = 8 in.
height = 5 in.

_____

5. base$_1$ = 24.6 cm
base$_2$ = 9.4 cm
height = 15 cm

_____

6. base$_1$ = 2.25 ft
base$_2$ = 4.75 ft
height = 3.5 ft

_____

Find the area of each triangle.

7.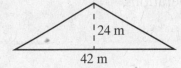
24 m
42 m

_____

8.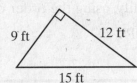
9 ft   12 ft
15 ft

_____

9.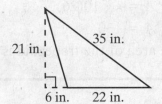
35 in.
21 in.
6 in.   22 in.

_____

10. base = 24 in.
height = 9 in.

area = _____

11. height = 27 cm
base = 34 cm

area = _____

12. base = 40 ft
height = 8.25 ft

area = _____

Find the area of each shaded region.

13.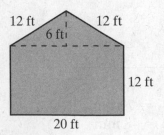
12 ft   12 ft
6 ft
12 ft
20 ft

_____

14.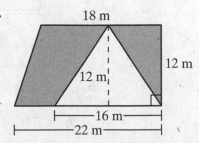
18 m
12 m
12 m
16 m
22 m

_____

15. A triangle has an area of 36 cm^2 and a base of 6 cm. What is the height of the triangle?

_____

Reteaching 10-3 *Area: Circles*

Find the area of the circle. Give an exact area and an approximate area.

The formula for the area A of a circle is $A = \pi r^2$, where r is the radius of the circle and π is a number that is close to 3.14, but not exactly 3.14.

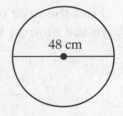

48 cm

In the circle shown, the diameter is 48 cm. The radius of any circle is half its diameter.

$\frac{1}{2} \cdot 48 = 24$

So, $r = 24$ cm.

$A = \pi r^2$

$A = \pi(24)^2$ Substitute 24 for r in the formula.

$A = 576\pi$ Simplify.

The exact area of the circle is 576π cm^2.

To find the approximate area, substitute 3.14 for π.

$A = 576\pi \approx 576(3.14) = 1{,}808.64$

Note: The symbol $\approx$ is read "is approximately equal to."

The approximate area is 1,808.64 cm^2.

Find the area of each circle. Give an exact area and an approximate area to the nearest tenth.

1.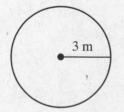

3 m

2.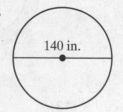

140 in.

3.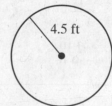

4.5 ft

$A = $ _____ $A = $ _____ $A = $ _____

$A \approx $ _____ $A \approx $ _____ $A \approx $ _____

4. $r = 15$ cm   **5.** $d = 16$ in.   **6.** $d = 7$ m

$A = $ _____ $A = $ _____ $A = $ _____

$A \approx $ _____ $A \approx $ _____ $A \approx $ _____

7. $r = 3.4$ ft   **8.** $d = 29$ cm   **9.** $d = 284$ mi

$A = $ _____ $A = $ _____ $A = $ _____

$A \approx $ _____ $A \approx $ _____ $A \approx $ _____

Practice 10-3 Area: Circle

Find the area of each circle. Give an exact area and an approximate area to the nearest tenth.

1. $r = 7$ m

A = _____

A ≈ _____

2. $d = 18$ cm

A = _____

A ≈ _____

3. $d = 42$ m

A = _____

A ≈ _____

4. $r = 35$ km

A = _____

A ≈ _____

5. $d = 22$ cm

A = _____

A ≈ _____

6. $r = 25$ ft

A = _____

A ≈ _____

7. $r = 3\frac{1}{2}$ mi

A = _____

A ≈ _____

8. $d = 5$ in.

A = _____

A ≈ _____

9. $d = 9.8$ mm

A = _____

A ≈ _____

Find the area of each shaded region to the nearest tenth.

10.

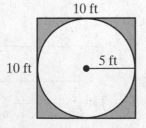

8 m   8 m

12 m

_____

11.

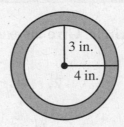

3 in.

4 in.

_____

12.

10 ft

10 ft   5 ft

_____

13.

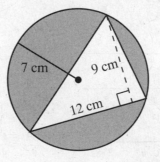

7 cm   9 cm

12 cm

_____

14. A goat is tethered to a stake in the ground with a 5-m rope. The goat can graze to the full length of the rope a full 360° around the stake. How much area does the goat have in which to graze?

_____

Reteaching 10-4 Space Figures

Name the space figure you can form from the net.

The net has a square and four triangles. So, the square must be the base. A pyramid has triangular sides and only one base. So, the net is for a triangular pyramid. You might try to picture what the figure looks like when it is cut out and folded. See the space figure at the right.

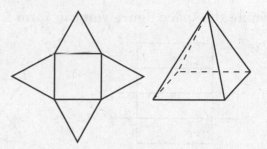

Name the space figure you can form from each net. Start by naming the polygons in the net.

1.

polygons: _____

space figure: _____

2.

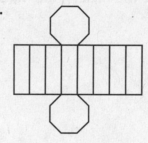

polygons: _____

space figure: _____

3.

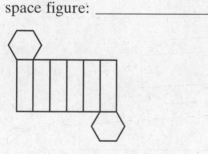

polygons: _____

space figure: _____

4.

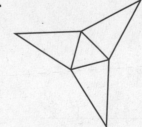

polygons: _____

space figure: _____

Practice 10-4 Space Figures

Name the space figure you can form from each net.

1.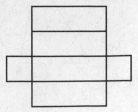

2.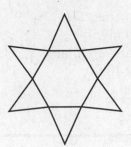

3.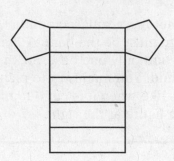

_____   _____   _____

For each figure, describe the base(s) and name the figure.

4.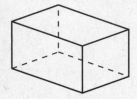

5.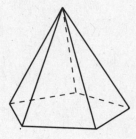

_____

_____   _____

6.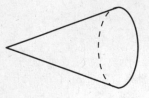

7.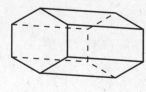

_____   _____

_____   _____

8.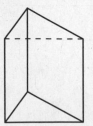

9.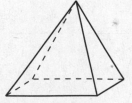

_____   _____

_____   _____

Reteaching 10-5 Surface Area: Prisms and Cylinders

Find the surface area of the triangular prism.
Two methods can be used to find the surface area.

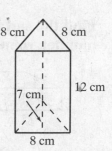

Method 1

Draw a net for the prism, find the area of each polygon in the net, and then add them together.

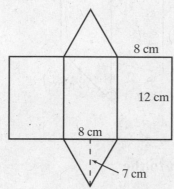

The triangles have area:

$A = \frac{1}{2}bh = \frac{1}{2}(8)7 = 28 \text{ cm}^2$

Each rectangle has area:

$A = bh = 8(12) = 96 \text{ cm}^2$

The total area of the 2 triangles and 3 rectangles is:

$28 + 28 + 96 + 96 + 96 = 344 \text{ cm}^2$

Method 2

Use the formula

$\text{S.A.} = \text{L.A.} + 2B$

$\text{L.A.} = ph$

$p = 3(8) = 24$

$\text{L.A.} = 24(12) = 288 \text{ cm}^2$

$B = \frac{1}{2}bh = \frac{1}{2}(8)(7) = 28 \text{ cm}^2$

$\text{S.A.} = \text{L.A.} + 2B$

$\quad\quad = 288 + 2(28)$

$\quad\quad = 344 \text{ cm}^2$

Find the surface area of each prism using the method you prefer.

1.
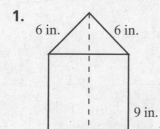

2.
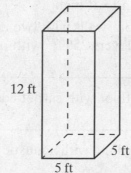

3.
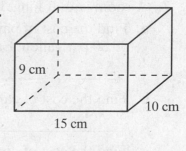

_____   _____   _____

Practice 10-5 Surface Area: Prisms and Cylinders

Find the surface area of each space figure. If the answer is not a whole number, round to the nearest tenth.

1.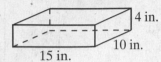
4 in.
10 in.
15 in.

2.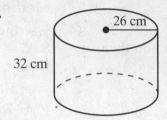
26 cm
32 cm

3.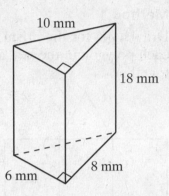
10 mm
18 mm
6 mm
8 mm

_____ _____ _____

Find the surface area of the space figure represented by each net to the nearest square unit.

4.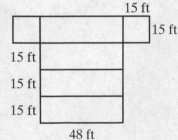
15 ft
15 ft
15 ft
15 ft
15 ft
48 ft

5.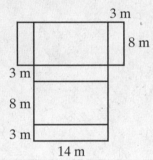
3 m
8 m
3 m
8 m
3 m
14 m

6.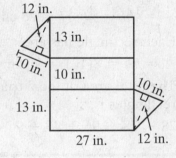
12 in.
13 in.
10 in.
10 in.
10 in.
13 in.
27 in.   12 in.

_____ _____ _____

7. A room is 18 ft long, 14 ft wide, and 8 ft high.

   a. Find the cost of painting the four walls with two coats of paint costing
   $9.50 per gallon. Each gallon covers 256 ft^2 with one coat.

   _____

   b. Find the cost of carpeting the floor with carpet costing $5/ft^2.

   _____

   c. Find the cost of covering the ceiling with acoustic tile costing $7.50/ft^2.

   _____

   d. Find the total cost of renovating the walls, floor, and ceiling.

   _____

Reteaching 10-6 Surface Area: Pyramids, Cones, and Spheres

Find the surface area of the cone.

The formula for the surface area (S.A.) of a cone is S.A. = L.A. + B, where B is the area of the base and L.A. is the lateral surface area.

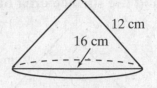

L.A. = $\pi r l$, where r is the radius of the cone and l is the slant height.

In the cone, given $r = \frac{1}{2}(16) = 8$ and $l = 12$:

L.A. = $\pi r l$

$\quad$ = $\pi(8)(12)$ $\qquad$ Substitute 8 for r and 12 for l.

$\quad \approx 301.44$ $\qquad$ Use 3.14 for π.

The base is a circle, so $B = \pi r^2$.

$B = \pi r^2 = \pi(8)^2$ $\qquad$ Substitute 8 for r.

$\quad \approx 200.96$ $\qquad$ Use 3.14 for π.

Thus, S.A. = L.A. + B

$\quad \approx 301.44 + 200.96$ $\qquad$ Substitute 301.44 for L.A. and 200.96 for B.

$\quad = 502.4$ $\qquad$ Add.

The surface area is about 502 cm^2. Don't forget to use square units.

Find the surface area of each space figure to the nearest square unit.

1.
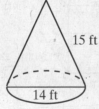
15 ft
14 ft

2.
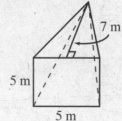
7 m
5 m
5 m

3.
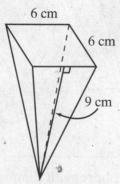
6 cm
6 cm
9 cm

_____ _____ _____

4. cone
$r = 10$ in.
$l = 14$ in.

5. square pyramid
$b = 11$ cm
$l = 8$ cm

6. cone
$d = 24$ m
$l = 25$ m

_____ _____ _____

▬ *Practice 10-6* Surface Area: Pyramids, Cones, and Spheres

Find the surface area of each space figure to the nearest square unit.

1.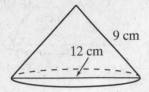
9 cm
12 cm

2.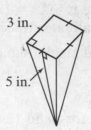
3 in.
5 in.

3.
22 m
20 m

_____ _____ _____

4.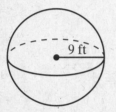
9 ft

5.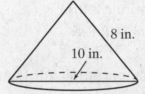
8 in.
10 in.

6.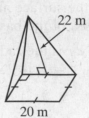
22 cm

_____ _____ _____

7.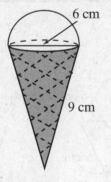
6 cm
9 cm

8.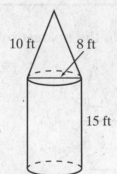
10 ft   8 ft
15 ft

9.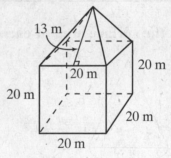
13 m
20 m
20 m
20 m
20 m
20 m

_____ _____ _____

10. a hemisphere with diameter 70 cm

_____

11. A cone and a square-based pyramid have slant heights of 6 in. The diameter for the cone and the base edge of the pyramid are both 8 in.

a. Which space figure has the greater surface area?

_____

b. By how much does the greater surface area exceed the lesser? Use 3.14 for π.

_____

Reteaching 10-7 *Volume: Prisms and Cylinders*

Find the volume of the cylinder.

$V = Bh$ Use the formula for volume.

$V = \pi r^2 h$ $B = \pi r^2$ since the base is a circle.

$r = \frac{1}{2}d = \frac{1}{2}(28)$ Find r from $d = 28$.

       $= 14$

$V = \pi r^2 h$

$V = \pi(14)^2(30)$ Substitute 14 for r and 30 for h.

   $\approx 18{,}463.2$ Multiply. Use 3.14 for π.

The volume is about 18,463 in.^{3} Don't forget to use cubic units.

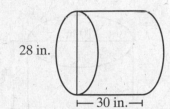

Find the volume of each prism or cylinder to the nearest cubic unit.

1.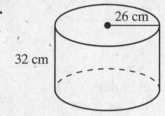

2.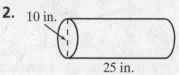

3.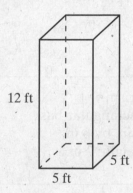

4.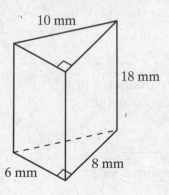

5.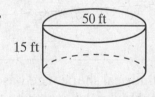

6.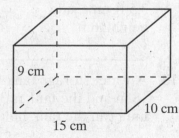

Practice 10-7 Volume: Prisms and Cylinders

Find the volume of each prism or cylinder to the nearest cubic unit.

1.
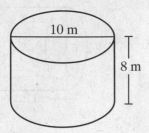
10 m
8 m

_____

2.
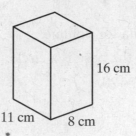
16 cm
11 cm   8 cm

_____

3.
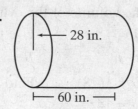
28 in.
60 in.

_____

4.
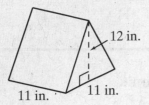
12 in.
11 in.   11 in.

_____

5.
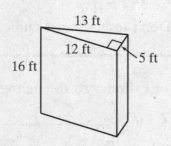
13 ft
12 ft   5 ft
16 ft

_____

6.
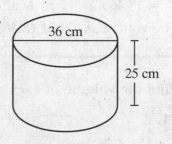
36 cm
25 cm

_____

7. prism
rectangular base:
8 in. by 6 in.
height: 7 in.

_____

8. cylinder
radius: 14 in.
height: 18 in.

_____

9. cylinder
radius: 5 cm
height: 11.2 cm

_____

10. prism
square base:
3.5 ft on a side
height: 6 ft

_____

11. cube
sides: 13 m

_____

12. cylinder
diameter: 5 ft
height: 9 ft

_____

13. A water storage tank has a cylindrical shape. The base has a diameter of 18 m and the tank is 32 m high. How much water, to the nearest cubic unit, can the tank hold?

_____

14. A tent in the shape of a triangular prism has a square base with a side of 8 feet and a height of 6 feet. What is the volume of the tent?

_____

▬▬ *Reteaching 10-8* Make a Model

Suppose you cut square corners off a piece of cardboard with dimensions 10 cm by 12 cm and fold up the sides to make an open box. To the nearest centimeter, what dimensions will give you the greatest volume?

Use a model to solve the problem. Cut out a 10 unit by 12 unit piece of grid paper. Cut a 1 by 1 square out of each corner. Fold to form a box.

The height of the box is the same as the length of the corner, 1 unit.

The length is 12 units minus the two corners or $12 - 2 = 10$ units. The width is 10 units minus the two corners or $10 - 2 = 8$ units.

$V = Bh = 10 \cdot 8 \cdot 1 = 80$ units^3

Now cut 2 by 2 squares out of the corners and fold the box.

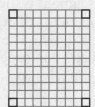

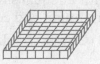

$h = 2$

$l = 12 - 2(2) = 12 - 4 = 8$

$w = 10 - 2(2) = 10 - 4 = 6$

$V = Bh = 8 \cdot 6 \cdot 2 = 96$ units^3

Now cut 3 by 3 squares out of the corners.

$V = (6 \cdot 4) \cdot 3 = 72$ units^3

Then cut 4 by 4 squares out of the corners.

$V = (4 \cdot 2) \cdot 4 = 32$ units^3

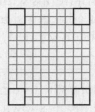

It is not possible to make a box by cutting 5 by 5 squares out of the corners. There would be no width.

So, to the nearest centimeter, a 2 cm by 6 cm by 8 cm box gives the greatest volume.

Suppose you cut square corners off a piece of cardboard with dimensions 12 cm by 15 cm to make an open box. Use a model to find the dimensions, to the nearest centimeter of each box. Record your work in the table.

	Length of side of corner	Length	Width	Height	Volume
1.	1 cm				
2.	2 cm				
3.	3 cm				
4.	4 cm				
5.	5 cm				

6. Which dimensions give the greatest volume? _____

Practice 10-8 Make a Model

Solve by making a model.

1. A narrow strip of paper is twisted once, then joined at the ends with glue or tape. The strip is then cut lengthwise along the dotted line shown.

   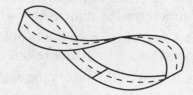

   a. Guess the results.

   _____

   b. Make and cut a model as directed. What are the results?

   _____

2. The midpoint of a segment is the point that divides the segment into two segments of equal length. A quadrilateral with unequal sides is drawn. The midpoints of the four sides are found and connected in order.

   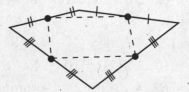

   a. Guess what kind of quadrilateral is formed.

   _____

   b. Draw four quadrilaterals with unequal sides and connect the midpoints of adjacent sides. What kind of quadrilaterals appear to have been formed?

   _____

3. A penny with Lincoln's head upright is rolled along the edge of another penny as shown in the figure.

   a. At the end, do you think Lincoln will be right-side-up or upside-down?

   _____

   b. Conduct an experiment to find out. What are your results?

   _____

4. A net for an octahedron is shown. All the sides are congruent, equilateral triangles. Cut and fold on the dotted lines. Find the surface area of the octahedron.

   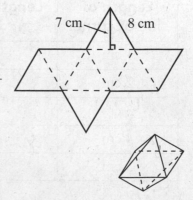
   7 cm 8 cm

▰▰▰ Reteaching 10-9 *Volume: Pyramids, Cones, and Spheres*

Find the volume of the cone.

Use the formula $V = \frac{1}{3}Bh$.

$r = \frac{1}{2}d = \frac{1}{2}(10) = 5$ The radius is half the diameter.

$B = \pi r^2$

$B = \pi(5)^2 \approx 78.5$ Substitute 5 for r to find the area of the base and multiply.

$V = \frac{1}{3}Bh$

$V = \frac{1}{3}(78.5)(11)$ Substitute 78.5 for B and 11 for h.

≈ 287.83 Multiply and round.

The volume is approximately 287.83 cm^3.
Remember to use cubic units.

10 cm
11 cm

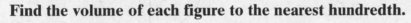

Find the volume of each figure to the nearest hundredth.

1.
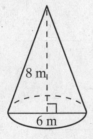
8 m
6 m

_____

2.
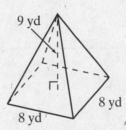
9 yd
8 yd
8 yd

_____

3.
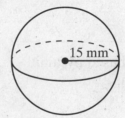
15 mm

_____

4. cone
$B = 93\ \text{ft}^2$
$h = 7\ \text{ft}$

_____

5. sphere
$r = \frac{3}{4}\ \text{in.}$

_____

6. pyramid
$B = 774\ \text{cm}^2$
$h = 42\ \text{cm}$

_____

7.
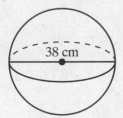
38 cm

_____

8.
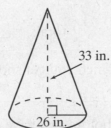
33 in.
26 in.

_____

9.
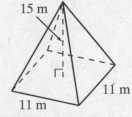
15 m
11 m
11 m

_____

Name _____ Class _____ Date _____

Find the volume of each figure to the nearest cubic unit.

1.

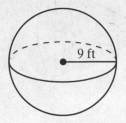

9 ft

_____

2.

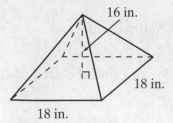

16 in.

18 in.

18 in.

_____

3.

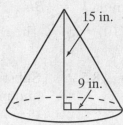

15 in.

9 in.

_____

4.

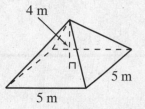

4 m

5 m

5 m

_____

5.

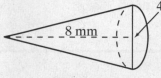

4 mm

8 mm

_____

6.

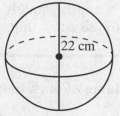

22 cm

_____

7. square-based pyramid
$s = 9$ in.
$h = 12$ in.

_____

8. cone
$r = 8$ cm
$h = 15$ cm

_____

9. sphere
$r = 6$ in.

_____

10. You make a snow figure using three spheres with radii of 12 in., 10 in., and 8 in., with the biggest on the bottom and the smallest for the head. You get snow from a rectangular area that is 6 ft by 7 ft.

a. Find the volume of snow in your snow figure to the nearest hundredth of a cubic inch.

bottom: _____   middle: _____

head: _____   total: _____

b. Find the area in square inches from which you get snow.

_____

c. How deep does the snow need to be before you have enough snow to make a figure? State your answer to the nearest $\frac{1}{4}$ in.

_____

Reteaching 11-1 Square Roots and Irrational Numbers

Estimate $\sqrt{27}$ to the nearest integer.

To estimate square roots, it is helpful to know the perfect squares in the following table.

n	1	2	3	4	5	6	7	8	9	10	11	12
n^2	1	4	9	16	25	36	49	64	81	100	121	144

Look at the n^2 row. These numbers are called perfect squares. Between which two perfect squares is 27?

$25 < 27 < 36$

so, $\sqrt{25} < \sqrt{27} < \sqrt{36}$

and $5 < \sqrt{27} < 6$

Since 27 is closer to 25 than to 36, $\sqrt{27}$ is closer to 5 than to 6.

Thus, $\sqrt{27}$ to the nearest integer is 5.

Each square root is between what two integers? Circle the integer to which it is closer.

1. $\sqrt{18}$ _____ , _____   2. $\sqrt{60}$ _____ , _____

3. $-\sqrt{8}$ _____ , _____   4. $\sqrt{90}$ _____ , _____

5. $\sqrt{29 + 8}$ _____ , _____   6. $-\sqrt{21}$ _____ , _____

7. $\sqrt{133}$ _____ , _____   8. $-\sqrt{118}$ _____ , _____

Estimate to the nearest integer.

9. $\sqrt{48}$ _____   10. $\sqrt{80}$ _____   11. $\sqrt{119}$ _____

12. $\sqrt{141}$ _____   13. $\sqrt{67}$ _____   14. $\sqrt{95}$ _____

15. $\sqrt{6}$ _____   16. $\sqrt{20}$ _____   17. $\sqrt{12}$ _____

18. $-\sqrt{3}$ _____   19. $\sqrt{42}$ _____   20. $-\sqrt{22}$ _____

21. $-\sqrt{110}$ _____   22. $-\sqrt{31}$ _____   23. $\sqrt{45}$ _____

Name _____ Class _____ Date _____

Practice 11-1 Square Roots and Irrational Numbers

Estimate to the nearest integer.

1. $\sqrt{18}$ _____   **2.** $\sqrt{24}$ _____   **3.** $\sqrt{50}$ _____

4. $\sqrt{8}$ _____   **5.** $\sqrt{62}$ _____   **6.** $\sqrt{78}$ _____

7. $\sqrt{98}$ _____   **8.** $\sqrt{46}$ _____   **9.** $\sqrt{38}$ _____

Simplify each square root.

10. $\sqrt{144}$ _____   **11.** $\sqrt{9+16}$ _____   **12.** $\sqrt{900}$ _____

13. $\sqrt{169}$ _____   **14.** $-\sqrt{100}$ _____   **15.** $\sqrt{0.16}$ _____

16. $\sqrt{\frac{16}{81}}$ _____   **17.** $\sqrt{\frac{4}{25}}$ _____   **18.** $\sqrt{\frac{121}{144}}$ _____

Identify each number as rational or irrational.

19. $\sqrt{289}$ _____   **20.** $5.7777\ldots$ _____

21. $\sqrt{41}$ _____   **22.** $0.62662\ldots$ _____

23. $\sqrt{49}$ _____   **24.** $\sqrt{52}$ _____

Find two integers that make each equation true.

25. $x^2 = 16$ _____   **26.** $3m^2 = 147$ _____

Use the formula $d = \sqrt{1.5h}$ to estimate the distance to the horizon d in miles for each viewer's eye height h, in feet.

27. $h = 12$ ft   **28.** $h = 216$ ft   **29.** $h = 412$ ft

_____   _____   _____

30. The Moon has a surface area of approximately 14,650,000 mi^2. Estimate its radius to the nearest mile.

_____

Reteaching 11-2 *The Pythagorean Theorem*

Find the missing length to the nearest tenth of a unit. The triangle is a right triangle. The side opposite the right angle is the hypotenuse and equals c in the Pythagorean formula. The other two sides are legs and equal a and b in the formula.

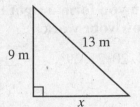

$a^2 + b^2 = c^2$	Use the Pythagorean Theorem.
$9^2 + x^2 = (13)^2$	Substitute 9 for a, x for b, and 13 for c.
$81 + x^2 = 169$	Simplify.
$81 - 81 + x^2 = 169 - 81$	Subtract 81 from each side to solve.
$x^2 = 88$	Simplify.
$x = \sqrt{88}$	Find the positive square root of each side.

Enter 88 then $\sqrt{}$ into a calculator.

The value is 9.3808315.

$x \approx 9.4$ Round to the nearest tenth. Use the sign $\approx$ for "is approximately equal to."

The length of x is about 9.4 m.

Find each missing length to the nearest tenth of a unit.

1.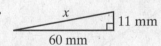

_____

2.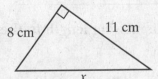

_____

3.

_____

4.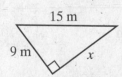

_____

5.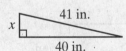

_____

6.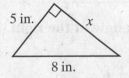

_____

Use the triangle at the right. Find the missing length to the nearest tenth of a unit.

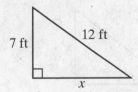

7. $a = 6$ in., $c = 14$ in.

$b \approx$ _____

8. $b = 22$ mm, $c = 25$ mm

$a \approx$ _____

9. $a = 31$ ft, $b = 55$ ft

$c \approx$ _____

10. $a = 16$ cm, $c = 28$ cm

$b \approx$ _____

▬▬ *Practice 11-2* The Pythagorean Theorem

Can you form a right triangle with the three lengths given? Show your work.

1. $20, 21, 29$ _____

2. $7, 11, 12$ _____

3. $10, 2\sqrt{11}, 12$ _____

4. $28, 45, 53$ _____

5. $9, \sqrt{10}, 10$ _____

6. $10, 15, 20$ _____

Find each missing length to the nearest tenth of a unit.

7.
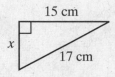
15 cm
x
17 cm

8.
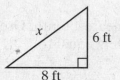
x
6 ft
8 ft

9.
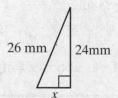
26 mm   24mm
x

_____

_____

_____

10.
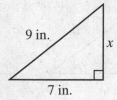
9 in.
x
7 in.

11.
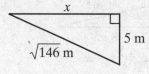
x
5 m
$\sqrt{146}$ m

12.
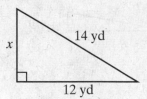
x
14 yd
12 yd

_____

_____

_____

Use the triangle at the right. Find the missing length to the nearest tenth of a unit.

13. $a = 6$ m, $b = 9$ m

$c \approx$ _____

14. $a = 19$ in., $c = 35$ in.

$b \approx$ _____

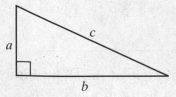
c
a
b

15. $b = 24$ cm, $c = 32$ cm

$a \approx$ _____

16. $a = 14$ ft, $c = 41$ ft

$b \approx$ _____

17. A rectangular park measures 300 ft by 400 ft. A sidewalk runs diagonally from one corner to the opposite corner. Find the length of the sidewalk.

_____

Reteaching 11-3 Distance and Midpoint Formulas

Find the perimeter of the figure. Round to the nearest tenth where necessary.

Use the distance formula to find the lengths of the sides.

$$d = \sqrt{(x_2 - x_1)^2 + (y_2 - y_1)^2}$$

First, find the coordinates of the vertices.

$A(-3, 2)$, $B(3, -1)$ and $C(-4, -4)$.

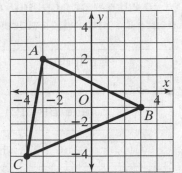

$AB = \sqrt{[3 - (-3)]^2 + [-1 - 2]^2}$ Replace (x_2, y_2) with $(3, -1)$ and (x_1, y_1) with $(-3, 2)$.

$\quad = \sqrt{6^2 + (-3)^2}$ Simplify.

$\quad = \sqrt{36 + 9}$ Find the squares.

$\quad = \sqrt{45}$ Add.

Similarly,

$BC = \sqrt{[3 - (-4)]^2 + [-1 - (-4)]^2}$ $AC = \sqrt{[(-3) - (-4)]^2 + [2 - (-4)]^2}$

$\quad = \sqrt{7^2 + 3^2}$ $\quad = \sqrt{1^2 + 6^2}$

$\quad = \sqrt{49 + 9}$ $\quad = \sqrt{1 + 36}$

$\quad = \sqrt{58}$ $\quad = \sqrt{37}$

The perimeter is the sum of the lengths of the sides.

perimeter $= \sqrt{45} + \sqrt{58} + \sqrt{37} \approx 20.4$

The perimeter is about 20.4 units.

Find the perimeter of each figure. Round to the nearest tenth when necessary.

1.

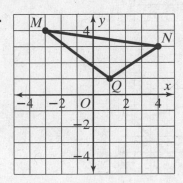

2.

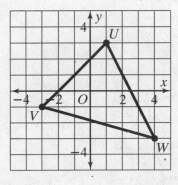

$MN = $ _____ $NQ = $ _____ $UV = $ _____ $VW = $ _____

$MQ = $ _____ $P \approx $ _____ $UW = $ _____ $P \approx $ _____

Name _____ Class _____ Date _____

Practice 11-3 *Distance and Midpoint Formulas*

The table has sets of endpoints of several segments. Find the distance between each pair of points and the midpoint of each segment. Round to the nearest tenth when necessary.

	Endpoints	Distance Between (Length of Segment)	Midpoint
1.	$A(2, 6)$ and $B(4, 10)$		
2.	$C(5, -3)$ and $D(7, 2)$		
3.	$E(0, 12)$ and $F(5, 0)$		
4.	$G(4, 7)$ and $H(-2, -3)$		
5.	$J(-1, 5)$ and $K(2, 1)$		
6.	$L(-3, 8)$ and $M(-7, -1)$		

Find the perimeter of each figure. Round to the nearest tenth when necessary.

7.
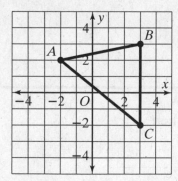

8.
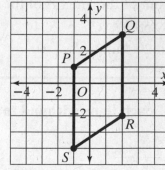

9.
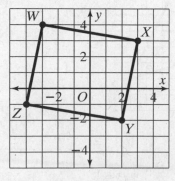

10.
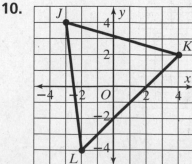

_____

_____

Reteaching 11-4 Write a Proportion

Write a proportion, and find the value of x given that
$\triangle ABC \sim \triangle CBD$.

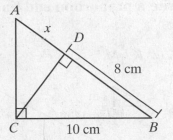

In similar triangles, corresponding sides are proportional. Thus, the
first step is to decide which sides are proportional and can be used
to find x. It is helpful to draw the triangles as separate figures.

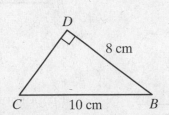

Notice that the right angles are $\angle C$ and $\angle D$. So $\angle C \cong \angle D$. The hypotenuses
are $\overline{AB}$ and $\overline{CB}$. So $\overline{AB}$ corresponds to $\overline{CB}$. The longer legs are $\overline{BC}$ and $\overline{BD}$.
So $\overline{BC}$ corresponds to $\overline{BD}$. You can also find these relationships in the
similarity statement.

So $\frac{AB}{CB} = \frac{BC}{BD}$ Write corresponding sides in each ratio. Write sides in
the same triangle in either the numerators or the
denominators.

$\frac{x+8}{10} = \frac{10}{8}$ $AB = x + 8, CB = 10 = BC, BD = 8$

$8(x + 8) = 10 \cdot 10$ Write cross products.

$8x + 64 = 100$ Use the Distributive Property.

$8x = 36$ Subtract 64 from each side.

$x = 4.5$ Divide each side by 8.

The length of x is 4.5 cm.

Write a proportion to find the value of each x.

1. $\triangle EFG \sim \triangle HJG$

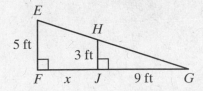

Proportion: _____

$x =$ _____

2. $\triangle KLM \sim \triangle LNM$

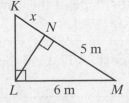

Proportion: _____

$x =$ _____

Practice 11-4 *Write a Proportion*

Write a proportion and find the value of each *x*.

1. $\triangle KLM \sim \triangle NPQ$

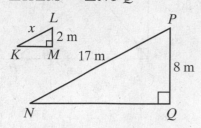

Proportion: _____

x = _____

2. $\triangle RST \sim \triangle RPQ$

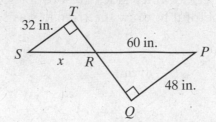

Proportion: _____

x = _____

3. $\triangle ABC \sim \triangle ADE$

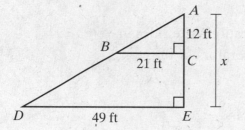

Proportion: _____

x = _____

4. $\triangle UVW \sim \triangle UYZ$

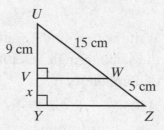

Proportion: _____

x = _____

Solve. Show the proportion you use.

5. A surveyor needs to find the distance across a canyon. She finds a tree on the edge of the canyon and a large rock on the other edge. The surveyor uses stakes to set up the similar right triangles shown. Find the distance from the tree to the other side of the canyon, *x*.

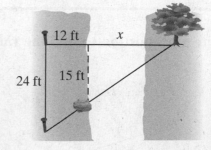

_____

6. Three cartons of juice cost $4.77. Find the cost of 8 cartons.

_____

7. If a pizza with a diameter of 12 inches costs $10.99, based on area, how much should a 15-inch pizza cost?

_____

Reteaching 11-5 Special Right Triangles

Find the length of each missing side in the figure.

$\triangle ABC$ is a 45°-45°-90° triangle.

$BC = AC = 8$ in.

$AB = AC \cdot \sqrt{2} = 8\sqrt{2}$ in. ≈ 11.3 in.

$\triangle ACD$ is a 30°-60°-90° triangle and $\overline{AC}$ is the shorter leg.

$AD = 2 \cdot AC = 2 \cdot 8 = 16$ in.

$DC = \sqrt{3} \cdot AC = 8\sqrt{3}$ in. ≈ 13.9 in.

Remember:

In a 45°-45°-90° triangle:
  leg = leg
  hypotenuse = leg$\sqrt{2}$.

In a 30°-60°-90° triangle:
  hypotenuse = 2 · shorter leg
  longer leg = $\sqrt{3}$ · shorter leg.

Find the length of each missing side in each figure to the nearest tenth of a unit.

1. $WZ =$ _____

2. $WX \approx$ _____

3. $WY =$ _____

4. $ZY \approx$ _____

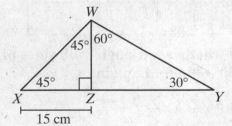

5. $LM =$ _____

6. $JM \approx$ _____

7. $JK =$ _____

8. $KL \approx$ _____

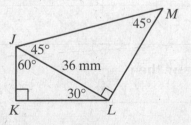

For 9–12, assume $RS = 7$ ft. Find the length of each missing side.

9. $RU =$ _____

10. $SU \approx$ _____

11. $ST =$ _____

12. $RT \approx$ _____

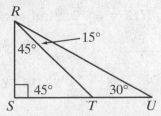

For 13–16, assume $SU = 11\sqrt{3}$ ft. Find the length of each missing side.

13. $RS =$ _____

14. $RU =$ _____

15. $ST =$ _____

16. $RT \approx$ _____

Practice 11-5 Special Right Triangles

The length of one side of the triangle is given in each row of the table.
Find the missing lengths for that triangle.

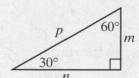

	m	n	p
1.	14		
2.			36
3.		$9\sqrt{3}$	
4.	5		

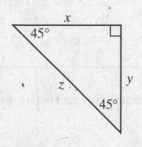

	x	y	z
5.	11		
6.		8.7	
7.			$7\sqrt{2}$
8.	17		

Tell whether a triangle with sides of the given lengths could be 45°-45°-90°
or 30°-60°-90°. Explain.

9. $3\sqrt{2}, 3\sqrt{2}, 6$

_____

_____

10. 10, 24, 26

_____

_____

In the figure, $BD = 6\sqrt{2}$. Find each value.

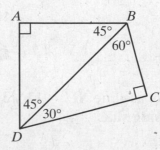

11. AB _____   12. AD _____

13. BC _____   14. CD _____

15. One leg of a 45°-45°-90° right triangle measures 14 cm.
Find the exact perimeter.

_____

Reteaching 11-6 Sine, Cosine, and Tangent Ratios

Find the sine, cosine, and tangent of $\angle K$.

The side opposite $\angle K$ is $\overline{JL}$.

The side adjacent to $\angle K$ is $\overline{KL}$.

The hypotenuse is $\overline{JK}$.

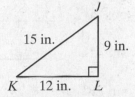

15 in. 9 in.

K 12 in. L

$\sin K = \dfrac{\text{opposite}}{\text{hypotenuse}} = \dfrac{9}{15} = \dfrac{3}{5}$

$\cos K = \dfrac{\text{adjacent}}{\text{hypotenuse}} = \dfrac{12}{15} = \dfrac{4}{5}$

$\tan K = \dfrac{\text{opposite}}{\text{adjacent}} = \dfrac{9}{12} = \dfrac{3}{4}$

Use $\triangle ABC$ for Exercises 1–6. Find each ratio.

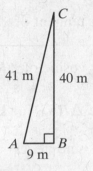

C

41 m 40 m

A 9 m B

1. sine of $\angle A$ _____ **2.** cosine of $\angle A$ _____

3. tangent of $\angle A$ _____ **4.** sine of $\angle C$ _____

5. cosine of $\angle C$ _____ **6.** tangent of $\angle C$ _____

Use $\triangle PQR$ for Exercises 7–12. Find each ratio in simplest form.

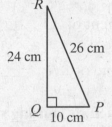

R

24 cm 26 cm

Q 10 cm P

7. sine of $\angle R$ _____ **8.** cosine of $\angle R$ _____

9. tangent of $\angle R$ _____ **10.** sine of $\angle P$ _____

11. cosine of $\angle P$ _____ **12.** tangent of $\angle P$ _____

Use $\triangle UVW$ for Exercises 13–18. Find each ratio.

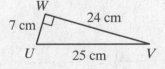

W 24 cm

7 cm

U 25 cm V

13. sine of $\angle U$ _____ **14.** cosine of $\angle U$ _____

15. tangent of $\angle U$ _____ **16.** sine of $\angle V$ _____

17. cosine of $\angle V$ _____ **18.** tangent of $\angle V$ _____

Practice 11-6 Sine, Cosine, and Tangent Ratios

Find each value. Round to four decimal places.

1. cos 20° _____

2. tan 64° _____

3. sin 41° _____

4. tan 8° _____

5. sin 88° _____

6. cos 53° _____

Use △MNP for Exercises 7 to 12. Find each ratio.

7. sine of ∠P _____

8. cosine of ∠P _____

9. tangent of ∠P _____

10. sine of ∠M _____

11. cosine of ∠M _____

12. tangent of ∠M _____

Use △RST for Exercises 13 to 18. Find each ratio in simplest form.

13. sine of ∠T _____

14. cosine of ∠T _____

15. tangent of ∠T _____

16. sine of ∠R _____

17. cosine of ∠R _____

18. tangent of ∠R _____

Write each ratio using square root signs. Use your knowledge of 45°-45°-90° and 30°-60°-90° right triangles.

19. tan 30° _____

20. cos 45° _____

21. sin 60° _____

22. cos 60° _____

23. tan 45° _____

24. sin 30° _____

25. A surveyor standing 2,277 ft from the base of a building measured a 31° angle to the topmost point. To the nearest ft, how tall is the building?

_____

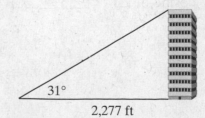

Reteaching 11-7 Angles of Elevation and Depression

A surveyor stands 38 meters from the base of a sheer cliff. Using equipment that sites from 1 meter off the ground, the surveyor measures the angle of elevation from her position to the top of the cliff as 58°. What is the height of the cliff?

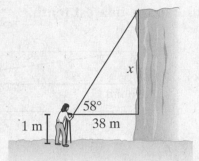

Start by drawing a diagram and labeling it with the information given. Label x in the right triangle. Remember the height h of the cliff is actually $x + 1$, since the surveyor is siting from one meter off the ground.

Determine what information is given. The angle of elevation is 58°. The side adjacent to the 58° angle is 38 meters.

The surveyor needs to determine x, the side opposite the 58° angle.

The tangent ratio uses the opposite side and the adjacent side, so use that.

$$\tan = \frac{\text{opposite}}{\text{adjacent}}$$

$\tan 58° = \frac{x}{38}$ Substitute 58° for the angle measure, 38 for the adjacent side, and x for the opposite side.

$38(\tan 58°) = x$ Multiply each side by 38.

$61 \approx x$ Use a calculator or a table.

$h = x + 1 = 61 + 1 = 62$ Add one meter for the tripod's height.

The cliff is about 62 meters high.

Find x to the nearest whole unit.

1.

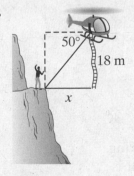

2.

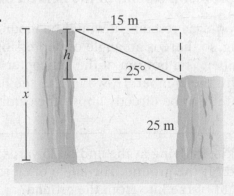

$x \approx$ _____ $x \approx$ _____

3. Thomas' kite is flying at the end of 82 feet of string. His end of the string is 3 feet off the ground. The angle of elevation of the kite is 55°. What is the height of the kite from the ground?

_____

Practice 11-7 Angles of Elevation and Depression

Find *x* to the nearest tenth.

1.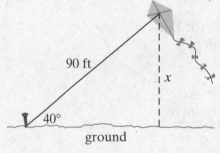

x ≈ _____

2.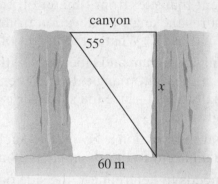

x ≈ _____

3.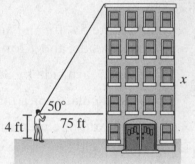

x ≈ _____

4.

x ≈ _____

Solve each problem. Round to the nearest unit.

5. A helicopter is rescuing a would-be mountain climber. The helicopter is hovering, so there is an angle of depression of 35° from the helicopter to the climber. The bottom of the helicopter's 12-meter ladder is hanging even with the climber. How far does the helicopter need to move horizontally to be directly above the climber?

_____

6. Kara's kite is flying at the end of 35 yards of string. Her end of the string is 1 yard off the ground. The angle of elevation of the kite is 50°. What is the height of the kite from the ground?

_____

7. Karl is standing 80 ft from the base of a tree. He sees the top of the tree from an angle of elevation of 42°. His eye is 4.5 feet off the ground. How tall is the tree?

_____

Name _____ Class _____ Date _____

Reteaching 12-1 *Frequency Tables and Line Plots*

Use the data in the rainfall table to make a frequency table and a line plot for Albuquerque.

Inches	0	1	2
Frequency	2	9	1

The numbers of inches are 0, 1, 2, so these are listed in the top row. Since two months have 0 inches (less than 0.5 in.), the frequency is 2. Albuquerque has one inch of rainfall in 9 different months, so the frequency is 9. Similarly, the frequency for 2 inches is 1.

To draw a line plot, start with a number line. Label 0, 1, and 2 inches. Then make the appropriate number of Xs above each number. Be sure to line up your Xs across from each other.

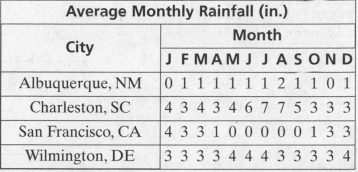

Average Monthly Rainfall (in.)													
City	Month												
	J	F	M	A	M	J	J	A	S	O	N	D
Albuquerque, NM	0	1	1	1	1	1	1	2	1	1	0	1
Charleston, SC	4	3	4	3	4	6	7	7	5	3	3	3
San Francisco, CA	4	3	3	1	0	0	0	0	0	1	3	3
Wilmington, DE	3	3	3	3	4	4	4	3	3	3	3	4

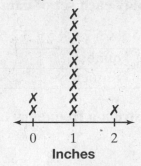

Albuquerque Rainfall

Inches

Use the data in the rainfall table to make a frequency table and a line plot for each city.

1. Charleston, SC

Inches					
Frequency					

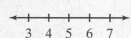

Charleston Rainfall

3 4 5 6 7

2. San Francisco, CA

Inches					
Frequency					

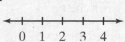

San Francisco Rainfall

0 1 2 3 4

3. Wilmington, DE

Inches		
Frequency		

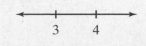

Wilmington Rainfall

3 4

Practice 12-1 Frequency Tables and Line Plots

Draw a line plot for each frequency table. Find the range.

1.

Number	1	2	3	4	5	6
Frequency	2	0	4	1	2	4

range: _____

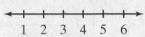

1 2 3 4 5 6

2.

Number	1	2	3	4	5	6
Frequency	4	4	0	0	3	2

range: _____

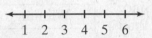

1 2 3 4 5 6

Display each set of data in a frequency table.

3. 5 1 4 6 2 6 4 5 1 3 2 6 4 5 4 6

Number						
Frequency						

4. 4 3 1 2 1 3 3 1 3 2 1

Number				
Frequency				

Construct a frequency table from the line plot.

5.

State Average Pupils per Teacher

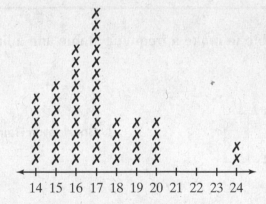

14 15 16 17 18 19 20 21 22 23 24

Pupils per Teacher										
Frequency										

6. What is the range in pupil-teacher ratios? _____

Reteaching 12-2 Box-and-Whisker Plots

Make a box-and-whisker plot for the data set.

Percent of Federally Owned Land in Ten Western States				
45%	24%	52%	61%	28%
42%	34%	48%	63%	36%

Step 1: First list the data in order from least to greatest. Find the median.

24 28 34 36 42 | 45 48 52 61 63

Since there is an even number of percents (10), there are two middle numbers. Add them and divide by 2.

$\frac{42 + 45}{2} = \frac{87}{2} = 43.5$ The median is 43.5.

Step 2: Find the upper and lower quartiles.

The lower quartile is the median of the lower half.   24 28 $\boxed{34}$ 36 42
The lower quartile is 34.

The upper quartile is the median of the upper half.   45 48 $\boxed{52}$ 61 63
The upper quartile is 52.

Step 3: Draw a number line. Mark the least and greatest values, the median, and the quartiles. Draw a box from the first to the third quartiles. Draw whiskers from the least and greatest values to the box.

The data range from 24 to 63. A scale of 5 from 20 to 70 would have 11 marks.

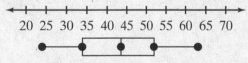

Make a box-and-whisker plot for each data set.

1. Area in 1,000 mi^2 of 13 western states.

122 164 71 98 84 147 114
111 98 85 104 71 77

   median: _____

   lower quartile: _____

   upper quartile: _____

   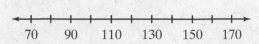

2. Percent of area that is inland water for 11 northeastern states.

13% 4% 26% 4% 32% 13%
15% 3% 21% 7% 21%

   median: _____

   lower quartile: _____

   upper quartile: _____

   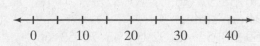

Name _____ Class _____ Date _____

Use the box-and-whisker plot to answer each question.

Weekly Mileage Totals, 24 Runners

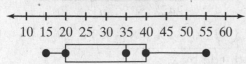

1. What is the highest weekly total? _____ the lowest? _____

2. What is the median weekly total? _____

3. What percent of runners run less than 40 miles a week? _____

4. How many runners run less than 20 miles a week? _____

Make a box-and-whisker plot for each set of data.

5. 16 20 30 15 23 11 15 21 30 29 13 16

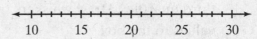

6. 9 12 10 3 2 3 9 11 5 1 10 4 7 12 3 10

7. 70 77 67 65 79 82 70 68 75 73 69 66
   70 73 89 72

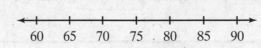

Use box-and-whisker plots to compare data sets. Use a single number line for each comparison.

8. 1st set: 7 12 25 3 1 29 30 7 15 2 5
            10 29 1 10 30 18 8 7 29
   2nd set: 37 17 14 43 27 19 32 1 8 48
            26 16 28 6 25 18

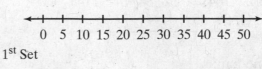

1st Set

2nd Set

9. Area in 1,000 mi²
   Midwestern states:
   45 36 58 97 56 65 87 82 77
   Southern states:
   52 59 48 52 42 32 54 43 70 53 66

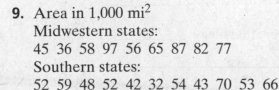

Midwestern States

Southern States

Reteaching 12-3 *Using Graphs to Persuade*

Use the data in the table. Draw a line graph on each grid at the right. Discuss the impressions given by the graphs.

U.S. Commercial Airline Traffic						
Year	1991	1992	1993	1994	1995	1996
Departures (millions)	6.8	7.1	7.2	7.5	8.1	8.2

The first graph gives the impression that airline traffic increased rapidly from 1991 to 1996. The second graph implies a much more gradual increase. The different impressions are given by the vertical scales. The vertical scale in the first graph is broken and increases by half millions. The vertical scale in the second graph is unbroken and increases by millions.

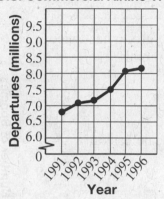

U.S. City Average Gasoline Retail Prices						
Year	1991	1992	1993	1994	1995	1996
Price	$1.20	$1.19	$1.17	$1.17	$1.21	$1.29

1. Make a line graph of the data in the table using the grid below.

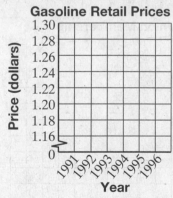

2. Make a line graph of the data in the table using the grid below.

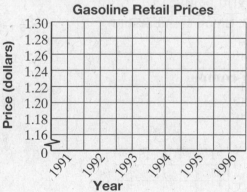

3. Compare the impressions given in the two graphs.

_____

_____

_____

Practice 12-3 Using Graphs to Persuade

Use the graph at the right for Exercises 1–5.

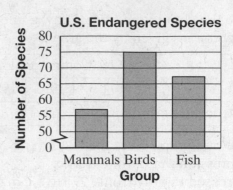

U.S. Endangered Species

1. Which group of animals appears to have more than twice as many endangered species as mammals?

   _____

2. Does one group actually have twice as many endangered species as mammals?

   _____

3. What gives the impression that one group has twice as many endangered species as mammals?

   _____

4. Redraw the graph without a break.

5. Describe the effect the change in scale has on what the graph suggests.

   _____

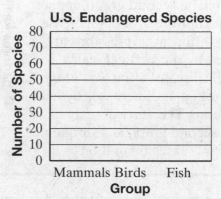

U.S. Endangered Species

Use the data in the table for Exercises 6–8.

U.S. Union Membership							
Year	1930	1940	1950	1960	1970	1980	1990
Union members (millions)	3	9	14	17	19	20	17

6. Draw a line graph of the data using the grid below.

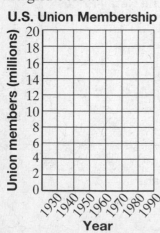

U.S. Union Membership

7. Draw a line graph of the data using the grid below.

U.S. Union Membership

8. What gives the different impressions in the two graphs?

   _____

Reteaching 12-4 Counting Outcomes and Theoretical Probability

A basketball team has 2 centers (C1 and C2), 2 point guards (P1 and P2), and 3 shooting guards (S1, S2, S3). Find the sample space and the probability that the first point guard (P1), starts a game if players for the 3 positions are chosen randomly.

You can use a tree diagram to find the sample space.

The tree diagram shows there are 12 possible outcomes. Of the 12 outcomes, 6 include P1:

C1-P1-S1, C1-P1-S2, C1-P1-S3
C2-P1-S1, C2-P1-S2, C2-P1-S3

$P(\text{P1 starts}) = \frac{\text{number of favorable outcomes}}{\text{number of possible outcomes}} = \frac{6}{12} = \frac{1}{2}$

You could also find the number of outcomes in the same space and the favorable outcomes with the Counting Principle.

2 center choices $\times$ 2 point guard choices $\times$ 3 shooting guard choices = 12

There are 12 possible outcomes. The favorable outcomes include 2 choices for center and three choices for shooting guard. However, only one choice for point guard is favorable.

2 center choices $\times$ 1 point guard choice $\times$ 3 shooting guard choices = 6

There are 6 favorable outcomes.

$P(\text{P1 starts}) = \frac{\text{number of favorable outcomes}}{\text{number of possible outcomes}} = \frac{6}{12} = \frac{1}{2}$

A basketball team has 2 centers (C1 and C2), 3 shooting guards (S1, S2, S3), and 3 power forwards (F1, F2, and F3). Players for the 3 positions are chosen randomly to start the game.

1. How many possible outcomes are there in the sample space?

   _____

2. List the sample space.

   _____

   _____

   _____

   _____

3. Find $P(\text{F2 starts})$. _____   4. Find $P(\text{S1 and F1})$ start.

Practice 12-4 Counting Outcomes and Theoretical Probability

A computer store sells 4 models of a computer (m1, m2, m3, and m4). Each model can be fitted with 3 sizes of hard drive (A, B, and C).

1. Find the sample space.

   _____

   _____

2. What is the probability of choosing a computer with a size C hard drive at random?

   _____

3. What is the probability of choosing a model 2 computer with a size A hard drive at random?

   _____

Solve each problem by drawing a tree diagram.

4. A ballot offered 3 choices for president (A, B, C) and 2 choices for vice president (M, N). How many choices for a combination of the two offices did it offer? List them.

   _____

5. The Cougar baseball team has 4 pitchers (P1, P2, P3, P4) and 2 catchers (C1, C2). How many pitcher-catcher combinations are possible? List them.

   _____

   _____

Solve each problem by using the counting principle.

6. There are 5 roads from Allen to Baker, 7 roads from Baker to Carlson, and 4 roads from Carlson to Dodge. How many different routes from Allen to Dodge by way of Baker and Carlson are possible?

   _____

7. Drapery is sold in 4 different fabrics. Each fabric comes in 13 different patterns. Each pattern is offered in 9 different colors. How many fabric-pattern-color combinations are there?

   _____

Reteaching 12-5 Independent and Dependent Events

You can select only two cards from the right. Find the probability both are T if you replace the first card before drawing the second and if you do not.

If you replace the first card before drawing the second, then the two events of drawing a card are independent. The first draw *does not* affect the second draw.

Use $P(A \text{ and } B) = P(A) \cdot P(B)$.

$P(T) = \frac{\text{number of favorable outcomes}}{\text{number of possible outcomes}} = \frac{3}{10}$

$P(2T) = P(T \text{ and } T) = P(T) \cdot P(T) = \frac{3}{10} \cdot \frac{3}{10} = \frac{9}{100}$

If you do not replace the first card before drawing the second, the two events of drawing a card are dependent. The first draw *does* affect the second draw.

Use $P(A \text{ and } B) = P(A) \cdot P(B \text{ after } A)$.

For the first draw, $P(T) = \frac{3}{10}$.

If the card is not replaced, there are only 9 cards left on the second draw.

If a T is drawn the first time and not replaced, there are only 2 T's left on the second draw.

$P(T \text{ after } T) = \frac{\text{number of favorable outcomes}}{\text{number of possible outcomes}} = \frac{2}{9}$

$P(2T) = P(T) \cdot P(T \text{ after } T) = \frac{\overset{1}{\cancel{3}}}{\underset{5}{\cancel{10}}} \cdot \frac{\overset{1}{\cancel{2}}}{\underset{3}{\cancel{9}}} = \frac{1}{15}$

So, with replacement, $P(2T) = \frac{9}{100}$ and, without replacement, $P(2T) = \frac{1}{15}$.

S
T
A
T
I
S
T
I
C
S

You randomly select a card from those above. You replace the card and select a second card. Find the probability of selecting each set of letters.

1. two Is _____

2. S and then I _____

3. C and then T _____

4. T and then S _____

You randomly select a card from those above and, without replacing the card, you select a second card. Find the probability of selecting each set of letters.

5. two Is _____

6. S and then I _____

7. C and then T _____

8. T and then S _____

Practice 12-5 Independent and Dependent Events

A shelf holds 3 novels, 2 biographies, and 1 history book. Two students in turn choose a book at random. What is the probability that the students choose each of the following?

1. both novels _____

2. both biographies _____

3. a history, then a novel _____

4. both history books _____

Meg flipped a penny the given number of times. What is the probability the results were as follows?

5. 2; two heads _____

6. 3; three tails _____

7. 2; a tail, then a head _____

8. 5; five tails _____

Two puppies are chosen at random from a box at the mall. What is the probability of these outcomes?

> **Free Puppies for Adoption!**
> 5 black retrievers
> 3 brown hounds
> 4 black setters

9. both black _____

10. both brown _____

11. a setter, then a hound _____

12. a retriever, then a setter _____

13. both setters _____

Are the events independent or dependent? Explain.

14. A guest at a party takes a sandwich from a tray. A second guest then takes a sandwich.

_____

_____

15. Sam flips a coin and gets heads. He flips again and gets tails.

You can select only two cards from the right. Find the probability of selecting a T and an N for each condition.

M	A	T	H
I	S
F	U	N

16. You replace the first card before drawing the second.

_____

17. You do not replace the first card before drawing the second.

_____

Reteaching 12-6 Permutations and Combinations

Ayla, Brandon, Juan, Li, and Marguerita want to go to see a ballet. They only have 3 tickets. How many ways can they choose the 3 that go? One way to solve the problem is to use the first letter of each student's name and list the combinations.

ABJ   BJL   JLM
ABL   BJM
ABM   BLM
AJL
AJM
ALM

There are 10 choices. You can also compute the number. There are 3 tickets. Five students want the first ticket. After one is chosen for the first ticket, only 4 want the second ticket. Then, only 3 want the third ticket. So, there are $5 \cdot 4 \cdot 3 = 60$ permutations. The 60 include different orders, like ABJ, BAJ, and JBA. However, in all cases, the same 3 students would be going to the ballet. Therefore, the *order doesn't matter*.

How many times are Ayla, Brandon, and Juan counted in the 60 permutations found?

ABJ   BAJ   JAB
AJB   BJA   JBA

Notice, each of the 3 is listed first. After one is chosen first, 2 can be listed second. After the first two are determined, only one is left for last. So, there are $3 \cdot 2 \cdot 1 = 6$ arrangements for each group of 3.

So, the five students have the following number of choices of 3 to go to the ballet.

$\frac{5 \cdot 4 \cdot 3}{3 \cdot 2 \cdot 1} = \frac{60}{6} = 10$ choices

---

1. How many choices would Ayla, Brandon, Juan, Li, and Marguerita have if they only had 2 tickets? _____

2. How many choices would the 5 students have if they had 4 tickets? _____

3. Three-digit numbers are to be formed using only the digits 1, 2, 4, 7, and 9. No digit may be repeated. How many different numbers can be formed? _____

4. An ice cream shop has 21 flavors. How many different two-dip cones can you have if the dips are not the same flavor? _____

Practice 12-6 Permutations and Combinations

Simplify each expression.

1. $_7P_2$ _____

2. $_7C_2$ _____

3. $_8P_3$ _____

4. $_9P_4$ _____

5. $_3C_2$ _____

6. $_{10}C_4$ _____

7. Art, Becky, Carl, and Denise are lined up to buy tickets.

   a. How many different permutations of the four are possible?

   _____

   b. Suppose Ed was also in line. How many permutations would there be?

   _____

   c. In how many of the permutations of the five is Becky first?

   _____

   d. What is the probability that a permutation of this five chosen at random will have Becky first?

   _____

8. Art, Becky, Carl, Denise, and Ed all want to go to the concert. However, there are only 3 tickets. How many ways can they choose the 3 who get to go to the concert?

_____

9. A combination lock has 36 numbers on it. How many different 3-number combinations are possible if no number may be repeated?

_____

Numbers are to be formed using the digits 1, 2, 3, 4, 5, and 6. No digit may be repeated.

10. How many two-digit numbers can be formed? _____

11. How many three-digit numbers can be formed? _____

12. How many four-digit numbers can be formed? _____

13. How many five-digit numbers can be formed? _____

14. How many six-digit numbers can be formed? _____

Reteaching 12-7 Experimental Probability

The table shows the colors of Lisa's baseball caps. Find the probability that a random cap from Lisa's collection is green or orange. Round to the nearest tenth of a percent.

$$P(\text{event}) = \frac{\text{number of times the event occurs}}{\text{number of trials}}$$

Since there are 30 caps in Lisa's collection, the number of trials is 30. Five caps are green and 3 are orange, so $5 + 3 = 8$ are either green or orange.

$$P(\text{green or orange}) = \frac{8}{30} \approx 26.7\%$$

Color	Number of Caps
blue	7
green	5
orange	3
white	9
red	6

Use the data in the table above. For each color, find the experimental probability that a random cap from Lisa's collection is that color. Write the probability as a percent, to the nearest tenth of a percent.

1. blue _____

2. green _____

3. red _____

4. red or white _____

5. blue or orange _____

6. not white _____

7. not green or red _____

8. pink _____

9. not pink _____

10. red, white, or blue _____

11. green, orange, or white _____

12. not green, orange, or white _____

Practice 12-7 Experimental Probability

The table shows the colors of Rahmi's soccer shirts. For each color, find the experimental probability that a random shirt from Rahmi's collection is that color. Write the probability as a percent, to the nearest tenth of a percent.

Color	Number of shirts
red	6
white	4
orange	3
blue	2

1. red _____

2. white _____

3. orange _____

4. blue _____

5. red or blue _____

6. not white _____

7. not orange or red _____

8. green _____

Your school's basketball team has an equal chance of winning or losing the first three games of the season. You simulate the probability by tossing a coin 60 times, letting heads stand for a win and tails stand for a loss. Use the data below. Find each experimental probability as a percent.

HHH THH THT TTH THH
HTH THH THH HTH HHH
THH TTH THH HTT TTT
HTT HHT TTH HTH THH

9. P(win all 3) _____

10. P(win exactly 2) _____

11. P(win exactly 1) _____

12. P(win none) _____

13. P(win at least 2) _____

14. P(win at least 1) _____

15. P(win less than 2) _____

Students were surveyed about the number of children living in their household. The table shows the results. Write each experimental probability as a fraction in simplest form.

Number of children	Number of students
0	0
1	11
2	15
3	3
4 or more	4

16. P(one child) _____

17. P(2 or more children) _____

18. P(at least 3 children) _____

Reteaching 12-8 Random Samples and Surveys

From 8,000 sports shirts produced, a manufacturer takes several random samples. Use the data in the table to estimate the total number of defective shirts based on Sample A.

Sample	Number Sampled	Number Defective
A	250	6
B	400	8
C	500	9

Set up a proportion.

$$\frac{\text{defective sample shirts}}{\text{sample shirts}} = \frac{\text{defective shirts}}{\text{shirts produced}}$$

$\frac{6}{250} = \frac{x}{8,000}$ Substitute.

$250x = 6(8,000)$ Find cross products.

$250x = 48,000$ Simplify.

$\frac{250x}{250} = \frac{48,000}{250}$ Divide each side by 250.

$x = 192$ Simplify.

The total number of defective shirts based on Sample A is about 192.

Use the data in the table above to estimate the number of defective shirts out of 8,000 based on each sample.

1. Sample B _____ proportion used: _____

2. Sample C _____ proportion used: _____

From 12,000 computer games produced, a manufacturer takes several random samples. Use the data in the table to estimate the total number of defective games based on each sample.

3. Sample A _____

     proportion: _____

Sample	Number Sampled	Number Defective
A	400	16
B	800	30
C	500	19

4. Sample B _____

     proportion: _____

5. Sample C _____

     proportion: _____

6. All 3 samples combined _____

     proportion: _____

Practice 12-8 Random Samples and Surveys

A school has 800 students. Two random surveys are conducted to determine students' favorite sport. Use the data in the table to estimate the total number of students who prefer each sport.

Sport Samples				
Sample	Number Sampled	Favorite sport		
		Basketball	Football	Baseball
A	40	16	14	10
B	50	22	16	12

1. basketball based on Sample A _____

2. basketball based on Sample B _____

3. baseball based on Sample A _____

4. baseball based on Sample B _____

You want to find out if a school bond issue for a new computer center is likely to pass in the next election. State whether each survey plan describes a good sample. Explain your reasoning.

5. You interview people coming out of a computer store in your town.

   _____

   _____

   _____

6. You choose people to interview at random from the city telephone book.

   _____

   _____

   _____

7. You interview every tenth person leaving each voting place in your school district.

   _____

   _____

Name _____ Class _____ Date _____

Reteaching 12-9 *Simulate a Problem*

Each carton of monster yogurt contains a card with a monster cartoon character on it. Each of the 6 characters is equally likely. You purchase 8 cartons of yogurt. Find the probability that you get at least 5 different cards. Simulate the problem.

Since there are 6 characters, you can use a number cube to simulate the problem. A trial consists of rolling the cube 8 times. The results of 5 trials are shown in the table.

In trials 1, 4, and 5, four different numbers were rolled, representing 4 different cards. In trials 2 and 3, five different numbers were rolled, representing 5 different cards.

So, at least 5 different cards were found in 2 of the 5 trials and the probability is $\frac{2}{5}$ or 40%. Note that "at least 5" means 5 or 6.

Trial 1	6 6 1 5 1 6 6 4
Trial 2	1 6 2 4 4 2 6 5
Trial 3	5 6 3 1 1 6 2 1
Trial 4	6 2 1 2 3 3 2 6
Trial 5	3 5 4 4 3 4 2 4

Use the table above combined with the one on the right to find each probability based on 10 trials. Write each probability as a percent.

Trial 6	5 6 1 1 5 1 1 3
Trial 7	2 4 4 6 5 6 2 6
Trial 8	2 4 4 2 2 6 6 4
Trial 9	1 4 6 4 4 2 3 4
Trial 10	4 4 4 2 4 5 3 6

1. Complete the frequency table for the ten trials.

2. Find the probability that you get exactly 4 different cards.

   _____

3. Find the probability that you get exactly 5 different cards.

   _____

4. Find the probability that you get at least 4 different cards.

   _____

5. Find the probability that you get at least 5 different cards.

   _____

6. Find the probability that you get no more than 4 different cards.

   _____

Number of Different Cards	Tally	Frequency (number of trials)
3		
4	III	
5	II	
6		

Practice 12-9 Simulate a Problem

Solve by simulating the problem.

1. Twenty people seated in a circle counted to seven, beginning with the number one. The seventh person dropped out and those remaining counted to seven again. If every seventh person dropped out, what was the number of the last person remaining in the circle? Use the number circle to simulate the problem.

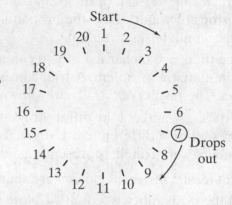

_____

2. The Rockets played their first volleyball game on Friday, October 18, and played a game every Friday thereafter.
   a. What was the date of their ninth game?

   _____

   b. What was the number of the game they played on February 7?

   _____

3. Five coins are placed side by side as shown. A move consists of sliding two adjacent coins to an open spot without changing the order of the two coins. (The move "2-3 right" is illustrated.) Find three successive moves that will leave the coins in this order: 3-1-5-2-4

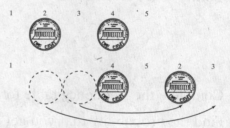

   _____

   _____

4. An irresponsible TV weatherperson forecasts the weather by throwing a number cube and consulting the weather key shown here. The weather during one 5-day stretch is given in the table. What is the probability that the forecaster was right at least 3 days out of 5? Use a number cube to simulate the forecaster's predictions. A successful trial occurs when you roll the correct weather three or more times out of five.

Weather Key
1–clear and warm
2–clear and cool
3–cloudy and cool
4–intermittent showers
5–continual rain
6–snow

Mon	Tue	Wed	Thu	Fri
continual rain	continual rain	clear and cool	cloudy and cool	snow

Work with a partner. Carry out 50 trials. Write the probability after the given number of trials.

a. 10 _____   **b.** 30 _____   **c.** 50 _____

Reteaching 13-1 *Patterns and Sequences*

Tell whether the sequence is *arithmetic*, *geometric*, or *neither*. Find the next three terms and write a rule to describe the sequence.

$9, 18, 36, 72, \ldots$

Find the difference between each term and the one before it to see if the sequence is arithmetic.

$9, \quad 18, \quad 36, \quad 72, \ldots$

$\underbrace{}_{\substack{18-9 \\ =9}} \underbrace{}_{\substack{36-18 \\ =18}} \underbrace{}_{\substack{72-36 \\ =36}}$

There is no common difference, so the sequence is not arithmetic. Find the ratio between each term and the one before it to see if the sequence is geometric.

$9, \quad 18, \quad 36, \quad 72, \ldots$

$\underbrace{}_{\frac{18}{9}=2} \underbrace{}_{\frac{36}{18}=2} \underbrace{}_{\frac{72}{36}=2}$

There is a common ratio of 2. The sequence is geometric. The rule is: *Start with 9 and multiply by 2 repeatedly*.

The next three terms are:

$$72 \cdot 2 = 144$$
$$144 \cdot 2 = 288$$
$$288 \cdot 2 = 576$$

$9, 18, 36, 72, \underline{144}, \underline{288}, \underline{576}$

Tell whether each sequence is *arithmetic*, *geometric*, or *neither*. Find the next three terms of each sequence. If the sequence is arithmetic or geometric, write a rule to describe the sequence.

1. $8, 11, 14, 17,$ _____ , _____ , _____ type: _____

rule: Start with _____

2. $4, 2, 0, -2,$ _____ , _____ , _____ type: _____

rule: Start with _____

3. $2, 10, 50, 250,$ _____ , _____ , _____ type: _____

rule: Start with _____

Practice 13-1 Patterns and Sequences

Tell whether each sequence is *arithmetic*, *geometric*, or *neither*. Find the next three terms of each sequence. If the sequence is arithmetic or geometric, write a rule to describe the sequence.

1. 7, 14, 28, 56, _____ , _____ , _____   type: _____

rule: _____

2. 5, 11, 17, 23, _____ , _____ , _____   type: _____

rule: _____

3. 32, 16, 8, 4, _____ , _____ , _____   type: _____

rule: _____

4. 25, 21, 17, 13, _____ , _____ , _____   type: _____

rule: _____

5. 9, 3, −3, −9, _____ , _____ , _____   type: _____

rule: _____

6. 8, 3, −3, −10, _____ , _____ , _____   type: _____

rule: _____

7. 2, −6, 18, −54, _____ , _____ , _____   type: _____

rule: _____

8. 1, 4, 9, 16, _____ , _____ , _____   type: _____

rule: _____

What is the common difference of each arithmetic sequence?

9. 16, 19, 22, 25, . . .   _____   **10.** 3, 5.8, 8.6, 11.4, . . .   _____

What is the common ratio of each geometric sequence?

11. 6, 24, 96, 384, . . .   _____   **12.** 12, 3, $\frac{3}{4}$, $\frac{3}{16}$, . . .   _____

Reteaching 13-2 Graphing Nonlinear Functions

Complete the table and graph $y = -2x^2 + 4$.

Substitute each value for x in $y = -2x^2 + 4$ to find the corresponding value of y.

x	$y = -2x^2 + 4$	(x, y)
−2	$y = -2(-2)^2 + 4 = -2(4) + 4 = -8 + 4 = -4$	(−2, −4)
−1	$y = -2(-1)^2 + 4 = -2(1) + 4 = -2 + 4 = 2$	(−1, 2)
0	$y = -2(0)^2 + 4 = -2(0) + 4 = 0 + 4 = 4$	(0, 4)
1	$y = -2(1)^2 + 4 = -2(1) + 4 = -2 + 4 = 2$	(1, 2)
2	$y = -2(2)^2 + 4 = -2(4) + 4 = -8 + 4 = -4$	(2, −4)

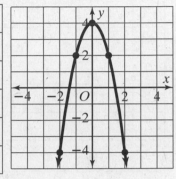

Plot the ordered pairs in the graph. The function is of the form $y = ax^2 + b$ so it is a quadratic function. The graph of a quadratic function is a U-shaped curve called a *parabola*. Connect the plotted points with a parabola.

A function of the form $y = a|x| + b$ is an absolute value function. The graph is V-shaped.

Complete the table and graph the function for the values in the table.

$y = 2|x| - 2$

x	$y = 2|x| - 2$	(x, y)
−2		
−1		
0		
1		
2		

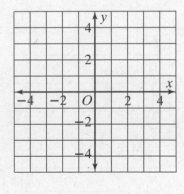

Practice 13-2 Graphing Nonlinear Functions

For each function, complete the table for integer values of x from -2 to 2.
Then graph each function.

1. $y = |x| - 2$

x	$y = |x| - 2$	(x, y)
-2		
-1		
0		
1		
2		

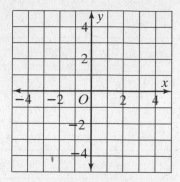

2. $y = -x^2 + 3$

x	$y = -x^2 + 3$	(x, y)
-2		
-1		
0		
1		
2		

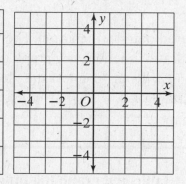

3. $y = 2x^2 - 4$

x	$y = 2x^2 - 4$	(x, y)
-2		
-1		
0		
1		
2		

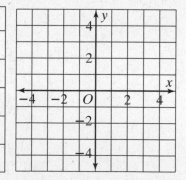

4. $y = 2|x| + 3$

x	$y = -2|x| + 3$	(x, y)
-2		
-1		
0		
1		
2		

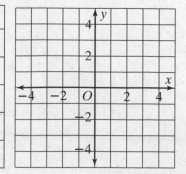

Reteaching 13-3 Exponential Growth and Decay

Complete the table and graph the function $y = 8\left(\frac{1}{2}\right)^x$.
Substitute each value of x into the equation and
find the corresponding value of y.

x	$y = 8\left(\frac{1}{2}\right)^x$	(x, y)
0	$y = 8\left(\frac{1}{2}\right)^0 = 8 \cdot 1 = 8$	(0, 8)
1	$y = 8\left(\frac{1}{2}\right)^1 = 8 \cdot \frac{1}{2} = 4$	(1, 4)
2	$y = 8\left(\frac{1}{2}\right)^2 = 8 \cdot \frac{1}{4} = 2$	(2, 2)
3	$y = 8\left(\frac{1}{2}\right)^3 = 8 \cdot \frac{1}{8} = 1$	(3, 1)
4	$y = 8\left(\frac{1}{2}\right)^4 = 8 \cdot \frac{1}{16} = \frac{1}{2}$	$\left(4, \frac{1}{2}\right)$

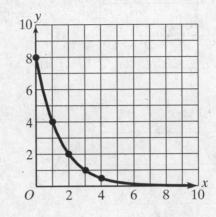

Plot the ordered pairs in the graph and connect them with a smooth curve.
Put arrows at the end of the curve to show it continues.

Complete the table and graph the function.

$y = \frac{5}{8} \cdot 2^x$

x	$y = \frac{5}{8} \cdot 2^x$	(x, y)
0		
1		
2		
3		
4		

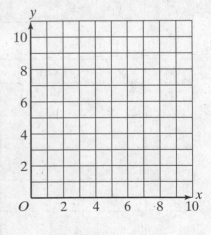

Practice 13-3 *Exponential Growth and Decay*

Complete the table for integer values of *x* from 0 to 4. Then graph each function.

1. $y = \frac{1}{3} \cdot 3^x$

x	y	(x, y)
0		
1		
2		
3		
4		

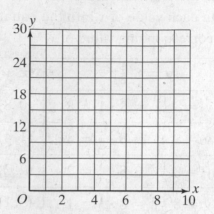

2. $y = \frac{5}{2} \cdot 2^x$

x	y	(x, y)
0		
1		
2		
3		
4		

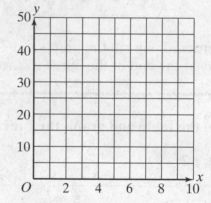

3. $y = 50(0.2)^x$

x	y	(x, y)
0		
1		
2		
3		
4		

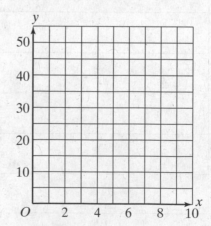

Is the point (3, 9) on the graph of each function?

4. $y = x^2$ _____

5. $y = 3^x$ _____

6. $y = \frac{1}{3} \cdot 3^x$ _____

7. $y = 3 \cdot \left(\frac{1}{3}\right)^x$ _____

8. $y = 3x$ _____

9. $y = x^3$ _____

Reteaching 13-4 Polynomials

The polynomial $d = 4.9t^2 - vt$ gives the distance d in meters an object has fallen after t seconds if it is thrown down with an initial velocity v. A rock is thrown from the top of a cliff with an initial velocity of 2 m/s. The rock takes 7.3 s to reach the bottom. To the nearest meter, how tall is the cliff?

$d = 4.9t^2 - vt$ Substitute 7.3 for t and 2 for v.

$d = 4.9(7.3)^2 - 2(7.3)$

$d = 4.9(53.29) - 2(7.3)$ Evaluate using the order of operations. Evaluate the power first.

$d = 261.121 - 14.6$ Multiply.

$d = 246.521$ Subtract.

$d \approx 247$ meters   Round.

Use the polynomial $d = 4.9t^2 - vt$ to find the distance each object falls for the given time and initial velocity. Round to the nearest meter.

1. $t = 7$ s, $v = 3$ m/s

_____

2. $t = 6$ s, $v = 3.5$ m/s

_____

3. $t = 5.7$ s, $v = 2$ m/s

_____

4. $t = 6.4$ s, $v = 2.8$ m/s

_____

Evaluate each polynomial for $x = -2$ and $y = 3$.

5. $x^2 - 2x - 5$

_____

6. $xy + y^2 + 2x$

_____

7. $9 - 3x^2$

_____

8. $x^2 - 2xy - y^2$

_____

9. The polynomial $S = 2\pi r^2 + 2\pi rh$ gives the surface area of a cylinder with radius r and height h. Find the surface area of a cylinder with radius 8 cm and height 14 cm, to the nearest cm^2.

_____

Practice 13-4 Polynomials

Evaluate each polynomial for $x = -1$, $y = 3$, and $z = 2$.

1. $x^2 + z$ _____

2. $3y + x$ _____

3. $2z + y$ _____

4. $x + y + z$ _____

5. $x^2 + y^2$ _____

6. $z - x - y$ _____

Evaluate each polynomial for $m = 21$, $n = -9$, and $p = 28$.

7. $3m - 2p$ _____

8. $2n^2 - 5m$ _____

9. $m^2 - n^2$ _____

10. $n^2 + 5n - 6$ _____

11. $5p^2 - 5p$ _____

12. $7m + 6p$ _____

Solve using the given polynomials.

13. Find the number of diagonals that can be drawn in a polygon with 24 sides.
$N = \frac{1}{2}n^2 - \frac{3}{2}n$
N = number of diagonals
n = number of sides

_____

14. A rock thrown from the top of a cliff at an initial velocity of 3 m/s takes 6.2 s to reach the bottom. To the nearest meter, how tall is the cliff?
$d = 4.9t^2 - vt$
d = distance fallen
t = time falling
v = initial velocity

_____

Tell whether each polynomial is a *monomial*, a *binomial*, or a *trinomial*.

15. $36abc$ _____

16. $10 - h^3$ _____

17. $95xy + y$ _____

18. $a^2 + b^2 + cd$ _____

19. $3k$ _____

20. $-12e + 12f^2$ _____

Reteaching 13-5 Adding and Subtracting Polynomials

Simplify $(5x^2 - 4x + 7) - (2x^2 - 3x + 12)$.

Add the opposite of each term in the second polynomial.

$(5x^2 - 4x + 7) - (2x^2 - 3x + 12)$

$\qquad = 5x^2 - 4x + 7 - 2x^2 + 3x - 12$ Write the opposite of each term in the second polynomial.

$\qquad = (5x^2 - 2x^2) + (-4x + 3x) + (7 - 12)$ Group like terms.

$\qquad = 3x^2 - x - 5$ Simplify. Notice $-4x + 3x = -x$. Write $-x$ as subtraction.

Simplify each sum or difference.

1. $(3x - 2) - (4x + 3)$ _____

2. $(2x^2 - 4x + 1) - (x^2 - 2x + 1)$ _____

3. $(2x^2 + 5x + 4) + (x^2 - 3x - 3)$ _____

4. $(-x^2 + 3x - 1) + (3x^2 - x + 2)$ _____

5. $(4x^2 - 3x + 8) - (3x^2 - 2x + 10)$ _____

6. $(2x^2 - 7x - 9) + (x^2 - 3x + 2)$ _____

7. $(y^2 - 8y - 6) - (y^2 - 10y + 3)$ _____

8. $(4xy - 2x^2 + 3y^2) + (x^2 - 5xy - 7y^2)$ _____

9. $(7x^2 - 5xy - 6y) - (3xy + 5x^2 - 11y)$ _____

10. $(6k^2 - 9) - (4k + 3)$ _____

11. $(8ab - 7b) + (6b - 9ab)$ _____

12. $(5x^2 - 7xy - 12y^2) - (5xy + 3 - 6y^2)$ _____

Practice 13-5 Adding and Subtracting Polynomials

Simplify each sum or difference.

1. $(10m - 4) - (3m - 5)$ _____

2. $(k^2 - 2k + 5) - (k^2 + 5k + 3)$ _____

3. $(2x^2 + 7x - 4) - (x^2 - 4)$ _____

4. $2x^2 + 4 + (3x^2 - 4x - 5)$ _____

5. $(-2x^2 + 4x - 5) + (8x + 5x^2 + 6)$ _____

6. $(3x^2y^2 + 2xy + 5y) - (-2x^2y^2 - 4x + 5y)$ _____

7. $(7x^3 - 5x^2 - 3x + 8) - (10x^3 - 4x^2 + 5x + 9)$ _____

8. $\begin{aligned} 2x^3 - 5x^2 \quad\quad - 5 \\ + \; 3x^3 + 7x^2 + 9x \end{aligned}$

   _____

9. $\begin{aligned} -4x^2y^2 + 3xy + x^2 - 4y^2 \\ + \; x^2y^2 - 6xy - x^2 - 5y^2 \end{aligned}$

   _____

10. $(x^2 + 2y + 5) - (4x + 4y)$

    _____

11. $(-4a^2b + 7ab^2 - 9a - 6b + 13) - (-6a^2b + 8a + 10b - 18)$

    _____

Write the perimeter of each figure as a polynomial. Simplify.

12.
$5m$
$2m^2 - 2$ $2m^2 - 3$

_____

13.
$2n + 3$
$2n - 3$
$3n - 4$ $7n + 2$
$n - 1$
$9n + 5$

_____

Reteaching 13-6 Multiplying a Polynomial by a Monomial

Use the GCF to write $36x^2y - 90x^2y^2$ as the product of two factors.
Multiply to check.

Write the prime factorization of each term to find the GCF.

$$36x^2y = 2 \cdot 2 \cdot 3 \cdot 3 \cdot x \cdot x \cdot y$$
$$90x^2y^2 = 2 \cdot 3 \cdot 3 \cdot 5 \cdot x \cdot x \cdot y \cdot y$$
$$GCF = 2 \cdot 3 \cdot 3 \cdot x \cdot x \cdot y = 18x^2y$$

Write each term as the product of $18x^2y$ and another factor.

$$36x^2y - 90x^2y^2 = 18x^2y(2) - 18x^2y(5y)$$
$$= 18x^2y(2 - 5y) \qquad \text{Use the Distributive Property.}$$

Thus $36x^2y - 90x^2y^2 = 18x^2y(2 - 5y)$.

Check by multiplying $18x^2y(2 - 5y)$.

$$18x^2y(2 - 5y) = (18x^2y)(2) - (18x^2y)5y \qquad \text{Use the Distributive Property.}$$
$$= (2 \cdot 18x^2y) - 5(18)x^2y \cdot y \qquad \text{Use the Commutative and Associative}$$
$$\text{Properties to rearrange terms.}$$
$$= 36x^2y - 90x^2y^2 \qquad \text{Simplify.}$$

The solution checks.

Complete to show how the given expression can be written as the product of two factors.

1. $5x + 5y = 5(\underline{\hspace{1cm}} + \underline{\hspace{1cm}})$

2. $-3m - 3n = -3(\underline{\hspace{1cm}} + \underline{\hspace{1cm}})$

3. $4x^3 + 4x^2y = \underline{\hspace{1cm}}(x + y)$

4. $6ab + 12b = \underline{\hspace{1cm}}(a + 2)$

Use the GCF of the terms to write each expression as the product of two factors.

5. $12x - 16y$ _____

6. $6a + 9b$ _____

7. $-9x^2 - 9y^2$ _____

8. $20m + 25n - 35k$ _____

Simplify each product.

9. $y(4x + y - 2x^2)$ _____

10. $3y(5y - 2x + 4xy)$ _____

Practice 13-6 Multiplying a Polynomial by a Monomial

Simplify each product.

1. $4x(3x - 5)$ _____

2. $-8x(x - 7)$ _____

3. $7xy^2(y - 2x + x^2)$ _____

4. $3xy(2xy + 5)$ _____

5. $-9xyz(-2xy + 3yz - 4xz)$ _____

6. $12ab\left(-\frac{1}{2}b + \frac{1}{4}a^3\right)$ _____

7. $-15a^2(a - b + 3c)$ _____

8. $-3x^2a^2(2a^3 + ab - x)$ _____

Write an expression for the area of each shaded region. Simplify.

9.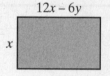

10.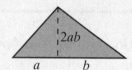

11.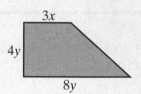

_____ _____ _____

_____ _____ _____

Use the GCF of the terms to write each expression as the product of two factors.

12. $8x + 8y$ _____

13. $13a - 13b$ _____

14. $2x^3 + 2x^2$ _____

15. $11a + 11b + 11c$ _____

16. $x^3y^2 + x^2y^3 + x^4y$ _____

17. $-12ab^2c + 18a^2bc^2 - 30ab^3c^3$ _____

18. $90w^3x + 144w^2$ _____

Reteaching 13-7 *Multiplying Binomials*

Simplify $(2x - 7)(x + 5)$.

$(2x - 7)(x + 5)$

$\quad\quad\quad = 2x(x + 5) - 7(x + 5)$ Use the Distributive Property, treating $(x + 5)$ as one number.

$\quad\quad\quad = 2x \cdot x + 2x \cdot 5 - 7 \cdot x - 7 \cdot 5$ Use the Distributive Property two more times.

$\quad\quad\quad = 2x^2 + 10x - 7x - 35$ Simplify.

$\quad\quad\quad = 2x^2 + 3x - 35$ Subtract $10x - 7x = 3x$.

So, $(2x - 7)(x + 5) = 2x^2 + 3x - 35$.

Simplify each product.

1. $(4x - 1)(2x + 7)$ **2.** $(x + a)(x + b)$

_____   _____

3. $(y - 9)^2$ **4.** $(x - 4)(x + 4)$

_____   _____

5. $(3m - n)(m + n)$ **6.** $(a - 14)(a + 8)$

_____   _____

7. $(k - 6)(k + 6)$ **8.** $(p + 5)^2$

_____   _____

9. $(a + b)(a - b)$ **10.** $(x + 1)^2$

_____   _____

11. $(a - b)(a - b)$ **12.** $(x + 4)(x - 4)$

_____   _____

13. A rectangle has length $4x + 3$ and height $3x - 7$. Find the area of the rectangle.

_____

Practice 13-7 Multiplying Binomials

Simplify each product.

1. $(x + 2)(x + 3)$

_____

2. $(x + 5)(x + 1)$

_____

3. $(x + 4)(x + 5)$

_____

4. $(x + 7)(x + 2)$

_____

5. $(x + 1)(x - 6)$

_____

6. $(x + 8)(x - 3)$

_____

7. $(2x + 5)(x + 3)$

_____

8. $(x - 4)(x - 6)$

_____

9. $(2x - 7)(2x + 7)$

_____

10. $(m - 15)(m - 20)$

_____

11. $(3k + 4)^2$

_____

12. $(x - 20)(x + 20)$

_____

13. $(5n + 4)(4n - 5)$

_____

14. $(10x - 1)^2$

_____

15. $(y - 7)(y - 6)$

_____

16. $(x - 9)(x - 5)$

_____

17. $(x - 10)(x + 3)$

_____

18. $(2x + 3)(3x + 2)$

_____

Find the area of each rectangle.

19.

$x + 5$

$x + 3$

20.

$4n + 7$

$3n + 2$

21.

$3h + 4$

$2h + 5$

_____ _____ _____

Reteaching 13-8 *Use Multiple Strategies*

A rectangular prism has length 5 cm, width $(x + 1)$ cm, height $(x + 3)$ cm, and volume 120 cm³. Find the width and the height.

To get a visual picture of the problem, draw a diagram. Label the dimensions. Next, write an equation.

$V = Bh$, $B = lw$, so $V = lwh$ Use the formulas for the volume of a prism and the area of a rectangle.

$V = lwh$

$120 = 5(x + 1)(x + 3)$ Substitute 120 for V, 5 for l, $x + 1$ for w and $x + 3$ for h.

$\frac{120}{5} = \frac{5(x + 1)(x + 3)}{5}$ Divide each side by 5.

$24 = (x + 1)(x + 3)$ Simplify.

Use Try, Test, Revise to find x. Organize tests in a table.

x	$x + 1$	$x + 3$	$(x + 1)(x + 3)$	Comment
2	3	5	15	Too low
4	5	7	35	Too high
3	4	6	24	$x = 3$

If $x = 3$, $x + 1 = 3 + 1 = 4$
$x + 3 = 3 + 3 = 6$

The width of the prism is 4 cm and the height is 6 cm.

Check: $V = 5 \cdot 4 \cdot 6 = 120$ cm³ ✓

Use multiple strategies to solve each problem.

1. The product of two whole numbers is 36. What is the greatest possible sum that the numbers can have?

_____

2. The sum of two numbers is 14. What is the greatest possible product that the numbers can have?

_____

3. A rectangle has length $k + 6$ and width $k - 6$. The area of the rectangle is 64. Find the length and the width.

_____

■ *Practice 13-8* *Use Multiple Strategies*

Use multiple strategies to solve each problem.

1. A rectangle has length $(x - 3)^2$ and width 4. The perimeter of the rectangle is 40. Find the length.

   _____

2. A rectangular prism has length $x + 2$, width $x + 1$, height 4, and volume 24. Find the length and the width.

   _____

3. A piece of cardboard measures 12 ft by 12 ft. Corners are to be cut from it as shown by the broken lines, and the sides folded up to make a box with an open top. What size corners should be cut from the cardboard to make a box with the greatest possible volume?

   _____

4. What size corners should be cut from a piece of cardboard that measures 30 in. by 30 in. to make an open-top box with the greatest possible volume?

   _____

5. What is the maximum number of small boxes that can fit inside the large box?

   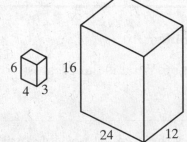

   _____

6. The perimeter of a right triangle is 24 in. Find the dimensions of the triangle if the sides are all whole-number lengths.

   _____